German Rocket Fighters

German
Rocket Fighters

of World War II

Hans-Peter Diedrich

Schiffer Military History
Atglen, PA

Translated from the German by Don Cox
Book Design by Ian Robertson.

Printed in China.
ISBN: 0-7643-2220-6

This book was originally printed under the title,
Die deutschen Raketenflugzeuge bis 1945
by Aviatic Verlag

For the largest selection of fine reference books on this and related subjects, please visit our website - **www.schifferbooks.com** - or call for a free catalog.

We are interested in hearing from authors with book ideas on related topics.

Published by Schiffer Publishing Ltd.
4880 Lower Valley Road
Atglen, PA 19310
Phone: (610) 593-1777
FAX: (610) 593-2002
E-mail: info@schifferbooks.com.
Visit our web site at: www.schifferbooks.com
Please write for a free catalog.
This book may be purchased from the publisher.
Please include $3.95 postage.
Try your bookstore first.

In Europe, Schiffer books are distributed by:
Bushwood Books
6 Marksbury Avenue
Kew Gardens
Surrey TW9 4JF
England
Phone: 44 (0) 20 8392-8585
FAX: 44 (0) 20 8392-9876
E-mail: info@bushwoodbooks.co.uk.
Free postage in the UK. Europe: air mail at cost.
Try your bookstore first.

Contents

Foreword

Every aviation enthusiast today can tell you that the rocket-propelled Bell X-1 broke through the sound barrier on 14 October 1947 and attained a speed of Mach 1.015 at the hands of pilot Chuck Yeager. But hardly anyone now remembers that the development of rocket-powered aircraft began in Europe, and at a much earlier date. Following initial trials with solid fuel rockets as boosters in the late 1920s and early 1930s, it was engineers such as Wernher von Braun and Hellmuth Walter, champions of developing suitable liquid-fueled rocket engines in Germany, and men like Lippisch and Heinkel, who integrated this new technology into airframe design, and in short order and often under the most trying circumstances, ultimately put these new rocket planes into the air. At the time, rocket propulsion for aircraft was also seen as a way of overcoming the speed limitations of piston-powered propeller-driven machines.

Unfortunately, many pilots sacrificed their lives over the course of these efforts and during subsequent operations. These sacrifices were in no small part due to the fact that this type of propulsion broached realms of speed approaching the magical sound barrier, something that had never before been achieved.

In America, development of rocket propulsion for aircraft did not really begin until around the end of the Second World War. The first U.S. rocket fighter, a tailless design, was the MX-324 Rocket Wing by Northrop. The Rocket Wing flew for the first time in July 1944 in Barstow, California. This aircraft thus became the sole American rocket fighter project that went into flight testing before the end of the war. Advances in German aviation technology in the area of jet propulsion (turbine and rocket-powered aircraft) at the time were of primary interest, and it is no wonder that the Americans understandably claimed these as spoils of war. This put them in the position of being the first to achieve supersonic flight as early as 1947, with both plane and pilot emerging unscathed. Not that the American aviation industry would not have been able to accomplish this on its own, but the technological "know how" of Germany's engineers undoubtedly played a part in ensuring this goal was achieved even earlier.

England was the first European nation to break the sound barrier on 9 September 1948, with the third prototype of the de Havilland D.H. 108 in a dive with pilot John Derry at the controls. This was also the first turbine-powered aircraft in the world to exceed the speed of sound. The second prototype of the D.H. 108 most likely also penetrated the sound barrier in September 1946, but the aircraft broke apart in midair, costing the pilot his life in the event. The first European pure turbojet fighter to break the barrier in horizontal flight was the French SFECMAS *Gerfaut*, on 3 August 1954.

The following chapters will examine the development of rocket technology, including such aircraft types as the He 176, Me 163 *Komet*, Ba 349 *Natter*, and the projects developed during the war's final days.

This should in no way deceive the reader into believing that rocket-powered aircraft did not see major or widespread use outside of Germany; rather, that in Germany rocket aircraft were much more quickly viewed as serving exclusively in the specialized role of point defense, and would very soon be replaced by the jet-powered designs looming on the near horizon.

After the war the U.S., Great Britain, and France all continued their efforts to develop a fast climbing interceptor using mixed propulsion. Examples of this are the Douglas *Skyrocket* and the French Sud-Ouest *Trident* fighter. The *Trident* was powered by a SEPR 481 liquid-propelled rocket (with three combustion chambers in the aircraft's aft section) and two Armstrong Siddeley Viper 5 turbine engines located at the wingtips. The *Skyrocket* was equipped with a Westinghouse J34-WE-22 turbine engine and a Reaction Motors XLR-8 rocket engine. Yet this development was very quickly overtaken by the new anti-aircraft missiles and the ever increasing performance of turbojet engines.

The United States subsequently continued using rocket-powered planes, albeit almost exclusively for high altitude speed research, as impressively evidenced by the X-2, and later the X-15. Prior to its crash, the second prototype of the X-2 was the first aircraft to attain a speed of Mach 3.3, and the X-15 achieved a hitherto unbroken maximum speed record of Mach 6.72 in October 1967.

Development of Rocket Technology in Germany

Looking at the development of rocket-powered aircraft in Germany—a field that reaches back into the second decade of the last century—one must first separate the development of pure rocket technology from the unique situation of German aviation following that country's defeat in the First World War. In doing so, however, one cannot overlook the interaction between such pioneers as Max Valier, Gottlieb Espenlaub, and others.

Rocket Development in Germany

Initial ideas for using rocket technology as propulsion for transportation began just shortly after the end of the First World War, and these ultimately led to such well-known publications as Hermann Oberth's "Die Rakete zu den Planetenräumen" (1923), Max Valier's "Vorstoß in den Weltenraum" (1926), and Oberth's "Wege zur Raumschifffahrt" (1929). All these books were expressions of a certain euphoria that not only increasingly gripped Germany, but was also felt in England, France, Russia, and the United States of America.

On 5 July 1927 about 20 "rocket enthusiasts" in Breslau established the "Verein für Raumfahrt, Breslau" (Society for Space Travel, Breslau). In just six months the organization boasted over 500 members. At first the club carried out experiments with swept-wing rocket models with a span of up to 1.5

Rocket test stand at Kummersdorf. (*Deutsches Museum Munich*)

meters and powered by solid fuel rocket engines. The organization subsequently urged Germany to experiment with rocket-powered aircraft, and was for its part financially supported by the industrialist Fritz von Opel. Founding members of the club included such notables as Prof. Hermann Oberth, Max Valier, and Wernher von Braun. By 1932 the organization moved its headquarters from Breslau to the up-and-coming science and technology center of Berlin.

But up until the end of the 1920s rocket research was of a purely civilian nature, since up to about this time propulsion concentrated almost exclusively on solid fuel. It was not until the rocket researchers increasingly turned to development of liquid-fuel rocket motors that the military's interest became aroused. Liquid-fuel rockets have the advantage in that they can operate independent of any external medium, and are therefore theoretically unrestricted in their potential altitude and speed. In addition, liquid fuel offers a much greater performance yield than solid fuel propellants.

On 23 June 1930 Rudolf Nebel (aircraft designer and rocket technician) and Klaus Riedel carried out the first successful burn tests of a liquid-fueled rocket exhaust system in Berlin. Two months later, at the Chemisch/Technische Versuchsanstalt (Chemical/Technological Test Center), the two conducted the first successful test run of a liquid-fueled rocket engine, with a burn time of 96.5 seconds. It was ultimately the results of this test that, in 1932, prompted the *Reichswehr* to significantly increase research in the area of jet propulsion at Berlin-Kummersdorf.

In 1930 Nebel and Riedel carried out launch tests with a rocket known as the MIRAK 1 (MiniRAKete 1) at the Berlin rocket field, which was operated by the Verein für Raumschifffahrt. That same year Rudolf Nebel established contacts within the *Reichswehr*, where he found a ready audience for his ideas. This ultimately led to Nebel opening the "Raketenflugplatz Berlin-Tegel" on 27 September 1930. This was a 4 km² area that included five permanent buildings and a rocket test stand. The first launch of a liquid-fueled rocket from Berlin-Tegel took place on 14 June 1931, rising to an altitude of 60 meters. One year later, in March of 1932 the MIRAK 3 rocket was launched from Berlin-Tegel, boosted by its 3 liters of fuel to an altitude of 4,000 meters. One of the developers of this rocket was the young Wernher von Braun.

Independent of these Berlin efforts, Johann Winkler and Max Valier began in 1927 to work on their first practical experiments with liquid-fuel rocket propulsion. Johan Winkler finally succeeded in launching the HW 1—a liquid-fueled rocket powered by methane and oxygen—from Dessau on 14 March 1931. A short time later he repeated the launch, this time at the Stettiner Haff. Using a reworked design of this rocket, he continued his launch experiments throughout 1932 at the Frische Nehrung, near Pillau, in East Prussia. On 6 October 1932 the HW 2 was able to lift off, but fell back to earth immediately after launch. A shortage of funding prevented Johann Winkler from continuing any further work.

Additional financial support was withheld following an unfortunate demonstration of the MIRAK 3 before members of the *Heereswaffenamt*. Wernher von Braun then became a liaison man to the *Heereswaffenamt*, and a short time later established a test center for liquid-fueled rocketry at Kummersdorf West under the command of *Hauptmann* Dornberger. One of his colleagues was Walter Riedel. The first test burn of a liquid-fuel system took place on 21 December 1932, albeit with an explosion. Three weeks later another test ran smoothly. A few months later the first complete Rakete A1 (Aggregat 1) was ready, with 300 kp thrust. However, the rocket suffered from aerodynamic instability, which was remedied with the improved design of the A2. In December 1934 two examples of these were successfully launched from the island of Borkum.

Building upon these results, von Braun proposed the construction of a lager rocket with 1,500 kp of thrust, the Model A3. Because of this rocket's dimensions—a length of 7.5 meters and a diameter of 75 centimeters—the missile was almost too large for the test stands at Kummersdorf West. Expanding the Kummersdorf site was out of the question, so the *Heer* and the *Luftwaffe* jointly decided in April 1936 to construct a high technology center for rocketry on the Baltic Sea island of Usedom. The *Heeresversuchsanstalt* (Army Test Center) at Peenemünde East would include an East Works and a West Works. The *Luftwaffenvesuchsanstalt* (Air Force Test Center) would be located at Pennemünde West, which operated its own airfield at Karlshagen.

By July 1937 the first scientists and engineers had moved to Peenemünde. In April 1938 the first airplane took off from the runway at Peenemünde West, and by the end of 1939 construction of the facilities had progressed to the point where the entire rocket development program could be moved from Kummersdorf to Peenemünde.

Ultimately, it was at Peenemünde East where Wernher von Braun worked on a rocket with 25 tons of thrust, later to become the A4, or the V2, as it was also known. And it was at Peenemünde West where,

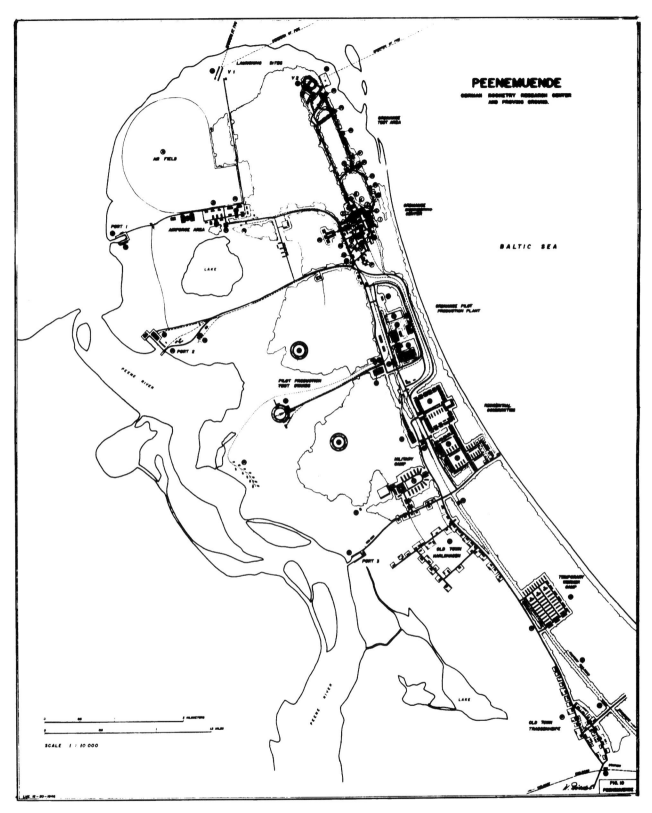

Layout of the Peenemünde rocket test center on the Usedom peninsula. (*Deutsches Museum* Munich)

Major sites associated with rocket technology in Germany.

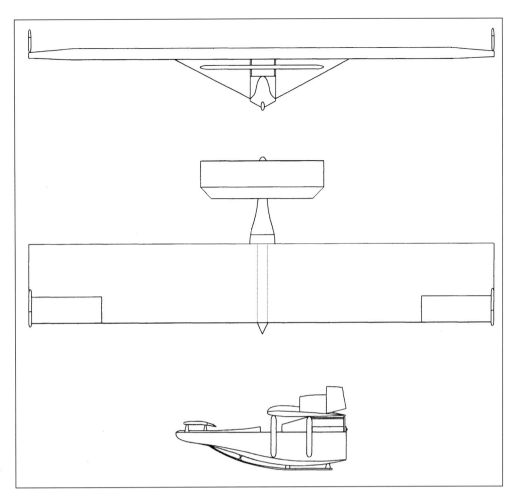

The DFS *"Ente"* experimental glider.

starting in December 1942, the Fieseler Fi 103 (aka the V1) was tested.

Hermann Oberth also worked at Peenemünde from 1941 onward. After the war he participated in the American space program alongside Wernher von Braun.

Deutsche Forschungsanstalt für Segelflug (DFS)

After the First World War Germany's enthusiasm for flying concentrated on gliding, an enthusiasm born out of necessity because of the ban on powered flight by the Allies. Experience quickly revealed that Germany offered two ideal areas for gliding: the updraft region around the Wasserkuppe, on the Rhön; and near Rossitten, on the Kurische Nehrung in East Prussia, where the first sailplane competitions took place as early as 1923/24.

On 31 August 1924 the Rhön-Rossiten-Gesellschaft (RRG) was established, uniting these two key regions of German gliding activities. The goal of this organization was to promote gliding, to include the testing of different designs and constructions, exploration of launch methods, and acceptance testing of

new aircraft types. As early as 1 April 1925 the research arm of the RRG was established under the name of the "Deutsches Forschungsinstitut für Segelflug" (German Gliding Research Institute) on the Wasserkuppe, under the direction of Dr. Walter Georgii. Technical director of the institute was Alexander Lippisch, who had been designing gliders and sailplanes on the Wasserkuppe since 1921 with a particular focus on tailless configurations.

Urged onward by rocket pioneer Max Valier and supported by rocket builder Sander and Fritz von Opel, Rhön pioneer Fritz Stamer (later director of flight operations within the DFS) began experiments using rocket propulsion for aircraft in cooperation with Alexander Lippisch. An acceptable test platform was found in Alexander Lippisch's experimental *Ente* glider design, which the RRG made available. The static stability of the *Ente* was greater than that of the tailless models, and the resulting acceleration forces could be better offset with this aircraft.

A first step was made on 10 June 1928 with a model from the *Storch* series, which was used in various general experiments on aircraft powered by solid

13

fuel rockets. To this end, the Sander Company provided rockets having a thrust of 5 kp with a burn time of 30 to 40 seconds and booster rockets (later known as RATO packs) with a 175 kp thrust and a 3 second burn time. In experiments using the 5 kp rocket an elastic chord was used to launch the aircraft. The first flights were made to set the trim on the model aircraft for level flight, thus making possible a subsequent launch with the 175 kp rocket motor. During the last flights with the booster rocket the model achieved a speed of nearly 500 km/h (according to a statement by Alexander Lippisch).

The time was now ripe for making the first manned flights in the RRG's *Ente*. Two solid fuel rocket engines were installed into the aircraft's aft tail. Originally, it was planned that the rocket compartment would be an enclosed area made of metal alloy, but the Opel Company delivered a simple open construction that was incorporated into the design. The two rockets could be electronically ignited one after the other from the pilot's seat. For the flight itself, the Sanger Company made available solid fuel rockets with thrusts ranging from 12 to 20 kp and a burn time of about 30 seconds. Furthermore, there were also booster rockets with a thrust of 360 kp and a burn time of 3 seconds, although it was ultimately decided to forego these, as the acceleration forces could not be determined with accuracy.

On 11 June 1928 Fritz Stamer took off from the Wasserkuppe in the *Ente*, powered by the Sander Company's rocket motors, on the first manned rocket-powered flight in Germany. The flight covered an overall distance of 1,400 meters and lasted a total of 70 seconds.

Fritz Stamer himself described the flight with the *Ente* in the magazine *Zeitschrift für Flugtechnik und Motorluftschifffahrt*, No. 12/1928, as follows:

"...First, two rockets with 12 and 15 kg each of thrust were fitted, which could be electronically ignited sequentially. The aircraft was launched with a rubber cord, like a glider.

The first takeoff was a failure, in that the airplane never rose off the ground and could not even be coaxed into the air when we ignited the 12 kg rocket.

Then we made the attempt using a 15 kg and a 20 kg rocket. With the 15 kg rocket the airplane successfully separated from the launch cord, but could not be kept in level flight and had to be brought down after about 200 meters in the air without ever being able to ignite the 20 kg rocket.

The third attempt made use of two rockets, each of 20 kg thrust. The airplane easily broke free of the ground with the launch cord and one of the rockets' thrust. After about 200 meters of level flight, during which I noted a light, constant climb of the plane, I banked to the right at an angle of about 45 degrees and again flew straight for about another 300 meters. I then made another right bank at about 45 degrees. The first rocket burned itself out just after this turn, and the second one was ignited, making continued flight possible. This time I flew approximately 500 meters in a straight line, followed by a right bank of about 30 degrees and then, after about 200 meters of straight flying on the new heading, landed the plane on gently rising ground just before the second rocket expired.

...After this attempt we made another one from a higher slope (training slope), the plan being to test a climb with two 20 kg rockets that would be ignited in tandem by an electronic switch, as before.

The rubber cord launch went smoothly, and as the plane rose I ignited the first rocket. After burning for just one or two seconds this rocket exploded with a loud bang. The 4 kg of black powder flew out and immediately caught the plane on fire. I slowly nosed the plane over, hoping to get the flames to dissipate, something which occurred after I'd lost about 20 meters of altitude. Once I made a smooth landing I tried to extinguish the fire. But since the insulation on the electrical wiring had burned through, the copper lines made contact and the second rocket ignited and burned itself out on the ground. Once it (the rocket - author's note.) had burned, the aircraft was completely doused."

Despite this abrupt end to the test flights, Stamer pronounced rocket propulsion to be entirely suited to aircraft, assuming appropriate safety measures were observed when installing rocket engines.

Gottlob Espenlaub ("Espe")

Gottlob Espenlaub was a cabinetmaker by trade. Following his passion, he built gliders and took part in the first Rhöne competitions on the Wasserkuppe.

It was also Gottlob Espenlaub who, together with Gerhard Fieseler, carried out the first towed flight in Germany on 13 March 1927 at Waldau airfield, near Kassel. That same year Espenlaub made a towed flight using a powered aircraft and a glider in Rossitten.

In 1928 Germany began experimenting with solid- and liquid-fuel rocket propulsion. Together with rocket pioneer Max Valier and Sander, Espenlaub carried out flight testing of his E-15 rocket-powered design. At this time, the solid fuel rockets were still a long way off from working reliably, and because of their extremely short burn times they were not an economical means of propulsion, either. It was not long before Espenlaub removed himself from the scene.

The E-15 was a tailless experimental design with a cantilever wing having a span of 12 meters with a slight sweepback. The airplane was fitted with a nose wheel, which was mounted backwards. The machine (empty weight of 220 kg) was powered by a 20 hp Daimler F7502 engine driving a tractor propeller. Thrust calculations were made before affixing solid fuel rockets to the wings.

Once the aircraft's flight handling characteristics had been determined with the propeller engine (first flight October 1929) technicians removed the Daimler engine, and in its place installed several Sander solid fuel rockets in the wing center section. These were rapid-burning solid fuel rockets of 180 kp thrust, which were to only be used for taking off. Less powerful (longer burning) 20 kp solid fuel rockets were planned for cruise flight. In the spring of 1930 test flights using rubber cord launches were conducted in Bremerhaven. The subsequent first flight under rocket power was also a successful one, but on the second rocket-powered launch Espenlaub accidentally ignited the more powerful booster rockets instead of the cruise rockets after the plane had already safely become airborne. As a result, the airplane nosed downward and scraped the ground, breaking up on impact. The result of this was that the widely advertised rocket open house flying day had to be canceled.

The Espenlaub E-15 during rocket test run. (*Deutsches Museum* Munich)

15

The Opel-Hatry 1 rocket plane taking off on its maiden flight at Frankfurt-Rebstock.

Opel's RAK 1 rocket-powered racing car (1928).

16

Fritz von Opel

From early on Fritz von Opel recognized Germany's growing euphoria with the idea of space travel, and also that of the positive image effect of public rocket events, which is why he subsequently became increasingly involved as a promoter of rocket propulsion technology. And, of course, it would also improve his name recognition, as well as that of his company. Nowadays it would be described as a remarkably successful public relations campaign.

So it was that, in 1929, Fritz von Opel had *Dipl. Ing.* Hatry build him an airplane that would be powered by Sander Company solid fuel rockets. Hatry designed a sailplane with a tube frame structure and an enclosed boat-shaped cockpit. The back wall housed 16 solid fuel rocket motors, each with 25 kp of thrust. These rockets were bundled in groups of four and ignited sequentially, so that a steady 100 kp of thrust could be maintained. This sequential ignition of the bundles was necessary since the rocket motors had such a short burn time, but the airplane needed a longer lasting thrust period for acceleration on takeoff. The airplane was fitted with dual rudders mounted on two separate booms to avoid the hot rocket exhaust gases. On 30 September 1929 Fritz von Opel, after two failed takeoff attempts, took off in the Opel-Sander RAK 1 (also often referred to as the Opel-Hatry 1) rocket-powered glider on its maiden flight from the

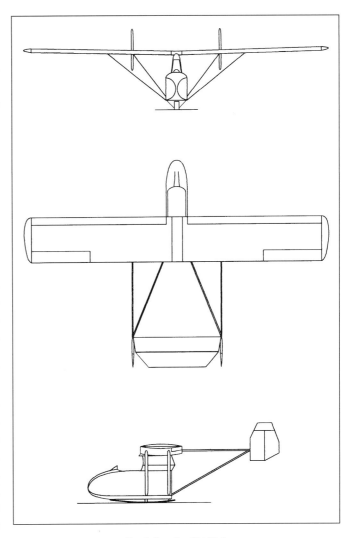

Opel-Sander RAK 1.

Record-setting run of the Opel RAK II rocket-powered racer at Berlin's Avus track.

17

airfield at Frankfurt-Rebstock. The flight covered a distance of 1,525 meters, with Fritz von Opel reaching a speed of 153 km/h. After this successful flight more powerful rockets were fitted, but the airplane was lost during the testing of these.

Another rocket project financed by Opel was the RAK 2 rocket-powered car. Powered by 24 solid fuel rocket engines ignited in tandem, on 23 May 1928 it attained a speed of over 200 km/h at the Berliner Avus track with Fritz von Opel at the wheel. Earlier, on 4 April 1928, the car was first successfully tested at the Opel test track. This project, too, developed under the direction of the rocket pioneer Max Valier.

Once Fritz von Opel achieved his economic goals, he again withdrew himself as a supporter of space travel.

Max Valier

Following a brief cooperative venture with Johann Winkler on the development of a liquid-propulsion rocket system, Austrian rocket pioneer Max Valier turned away from this approach, and instead experimented with solid fuel rockets made by the Sandler Company, which manufactured maritime emergency rescue rockets (high powered flares). He was backed financially in his efforts by Fritz von Opel. When Opel withdrew his financial support, however, Valier returned to liquid-fuel rockets. He found a potent new sponsor in the person of Dr. Paul Heylandt from the *Industriegasverwertung Berlin*, and began working on the development of a liquid-fueled rocket with the aid of Walter Riedel. However, during one of the first experiments with a combustion chamber for ethyl alcohol and oxygen, an explosion occurred on 17 May 1930 on the test bench at the Heylandt Works in Bretz, near Berlin, and Max Valier suffered fatal injuries.

It was also Max Valier whose enthusiasm in 1929 prompted Junkers to carry out experiments using solid fuel booster rockets (RATO) for aiding heavily laden aircraft on takeoff. Without these experiments, the record setting 10,000+ km flight of the Heinkel He 116R on 30 July/1 August would never have been possible, since the airplane was well overloaded with fuel on takeoff.

Opel RAK III rocket-powered rail car on 23 June 1928 at the *Reichsbahn* testing track in Burgwedel.

Heinkel

Heinkel He 112R

Ernst Heinkel seemed to always be working on building fast airplanes. But as early as the mid-1930s he recognized that propeller-driven piston-powered aircraft would soon reach their limits of speed. He personally estimated this limit to be around 750 km/h. He was ultimately proven correct through the long-standing (30 years) speed record set by Fritz Wendel with the Me 209 on 26 April 1939, at 755.138 km/h.

But Ernst Heinkel recognized yet another stumbling block for Germany's aviation industry, which he outlined in a 1935 memorandum entitled "Zur Frage der Motorenentwicklung" (On the Matter of Engine Development). In it, he showed that foreign development was superior to that of German as a direct consequence of the restrictions imposed following the First World War. He saw two solutions: either buy foreign technology for license manufacturing, such as with the BMW 132 radial engine—fundamentally a metric conversion of the Pratt & Whitney Hornet—or search for alternative propulsion options that would completely replace piston engines. It was this world view of Ernst Heinkel that ultimately led to the first turbojet powered aircraft in the world, the Heinkel He 178, taking to the air on its maiden flight on 27 August 1939 and ushering in the beginning of the jet age.

In November 1935 Ernst Heinkel made the acquaintance of Wernher von Braun. The latter worked at Berlin-Kummersdorf on the A1 rocket unit, a system which was expected to deliver 300 kp of thrust. Liquid oxygen and high concentrate ethyl alcohol served as its fuel. After many teething troubles the rocket motor had completed several test bench runs, and Wernher von Braun was of the opinion that it could be used as a supplemental propulsion system for aircraft. In addition to operational safety, a critical criterion for this type of propulsion is the control of the engine throughout the burn time. For a testbed, von Braun arranged for an old Junkers A 50 *Junior* to be provided by Walter Dornberger (council chairman of the RLM's ballistics advisory council). The rocket engine was affixed beneath the aircraft's belly, with the fuel tanks housed inside the fuselage, and a simple throttle was installed in the cockpit for the rocket system. Initially, ground tests were carried out at the Kummersdorf test facility. These resulted in several successful run-ups, each lasting 30 seconds. One major problem was the heat resistance of the combustion chamber material, which at the beginning could not survive anything longer than 30 seconds. Modifying the injection system solved the problem. But it was also discovered that the old Junkers A 50 airframe would not easily weather the stress of a more powerful rocket engine in flight. This meant that another testbed would have to be found.

This idea initially met with little sympathy within the *Luftwaffe, Heer,* and RLM, forcing von Braun to find himself another sponsor. He explained his situation to Ernst Heinkel, and Heinkel, always open to new ideas, showed an interest and promised his support to von Braun. Now the *Heereswaffenamt* (HWA) and the RLM became involved as well, since nobody wanted to be left out in the cold. As a result, in August 1935 the HWA, RLM, and Heinkel all signed a memorandum of understanding calling for von Braun to develop a liquid-fueled rocket engine at the HWA's Kummersdorf firing range and test it in a flying aircraft.

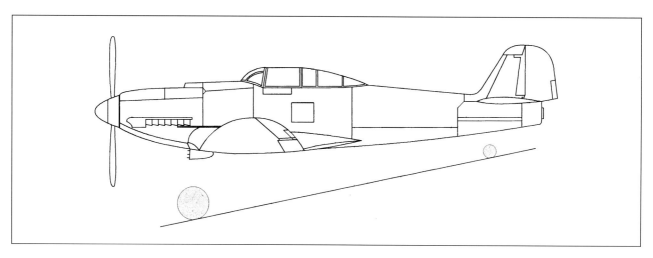

Heinkel He 112 R

Heinkel He 112 R

20

By early 1936 Heinkel had made available the airframe (inclusive of landing gear) of an He 112. Shipped to Kummersdorf, it was there used for fitting studies and thrust trials. The airframe was most likely the He 112 V3, *Werk-Nr.* 1292. In addition to the airplane Heinkel also sent along a team of technicians under the supervision of Walter Künzel, which accompanied the program its entire course. Furthermore, at the urging of former Heinkel test pilot Werner Junck, who at this time had a desk job within the RLM, a young Rechlin test pilot by the name of Erich Warsitz was detached to the program at the end of 1935, and began his work at Kummersdorf in early 1936. This brought the total number of personnel surrounding Wernher von Braun and Walter Künzel to 26 men.

Several ground runs were successfully carried out, including one in February 1936 in the presence of Ernst Heinkel. He saw a flame about 10 meters long shoot out from the back of the plane with a deafening roar. A few days later the airplane was completely destroyed when the combustion chamber exploded. One of the biggest problems stemmed from the fact that the rocket engine was originally designed for unmanned missiles, and was therefore laid out for a vertical takeoff. To function in an airplane, however, it had to be redesigned for horizontal flight, something that initially caused the lower part of the combustion chamber to repeatedly burn through. This was because the mixture concentration inside the combustion chamber was not homogeneously distributed throughout the chamber. It wasn't until the injection system was modified that this problem was alleviated.

Heinkel provided yet another He 112 fuselage, and ground trials resumed. This may have been the He 112 V4 (*Werk-Nr.* 1974). During these run-ups Erich Warsitz sat in the cockpit, and Wernher von Braun manually controlled the rocket motor. But this second airframe was also destroyed in a combustion chamber explosion. In the meantime, work had progressed to the point where both von Braun and Warsitz felt they could risk an airborne test. Both were able to persuade Heinkel yet again, and he eventually made available at his own expense a flight-ready He 112, the He 112 V5 (*Werk-Nr.* 1951). The rocket propulsion system was installed in addition to the piston engine. The tank for the liquid oxygen was located directly in front of the pilot's seat, and the round methyl-alcohol tank was fitted behind the seat, with the engine itself—to include the combustion chamber—integrated in the aft fuselage section. For the flight itself, the entire team relocated to the unused airfield of Neuhardenberg (about 60 km east of Berlin), at Oderbruch. This was a so-called operational field, with the runway's dimensions of 1,000 x 800 meters, and was only to be activated in the event of war. For this reason there was no kind of infrastructure whatsoever at the site. Buildings, test facilities, and airfield prepping were completed by the spring of 1937. The He 112R-VI, as the aircraft had been rechristened during the interlude, was transported to Neuhardenberg, where it was initially flown to speeds of up to 700 km/h in shallow dives. The He 112R was structurally reinforced to take the rocket engine and absorb the additional weight of both the engine and fuel, plus the anticipated higher speeds it would encounter.

After three successful ground run-ups in the He 112R-V1 von Braun, Künzel, and Warsitz decided to risk the first test flight on the following day. But this time, too, luck would not favor the team. During preflight preparations for the first flight the Jumo 210 piston engine blew up and destroyed the entire aircraft. Erich Warsitz survived the accident with only minor injuries and a lot of good fortune, for he and his seat were thrown out of the cockpit in the explosion.

But Warsitz was able to work on Ernst Heinkel for so long that he persuaded him to offer up yet another Heinkel He 112, this time an He 112B with a DB 600A engine. Just four weeks later, in April 1937, the aircraft had been converted to the He 112R-V2 and, after three problem-free ground runs, was ready for its first flight. Warsitz took off under piston power and climbed to an altitude of 450 meters, just under the cloud base. After flying an airfield circuit the necessary pressure for combustion had built up inside the oxygen tank (author's note: pressure buildup took place by evaporation of the oxygen in the tank; a backup pump or compressed air canisters were not available). Warsitz throttled the speed to 300 km/h and ignited the rocket engine.

There was such a kick that the speedometer jumped to 400 km/h in short order, then continued climbing. Then a bitter smoke began to fill the cockpit. Warsitz immediately suspected a malfunction in the rocket motor, which is why he throttled back on the piston engine in order to prevent the speed from building up even more. It was impossible to switch off the rocket engine; once ignited it burned nonstop until the fuel ran out. Warsitz jettisoned the canopy because of the smoke, but unbeknownst to him he had dropped to an altitude of 200 meters, making a bail-out impossible. In addition, he was most reluctant to abandon the valuable airplane. He therefore brought the plane in just above the ground and, the moment the rocket motor burned itself out, he pushed the airplane downward and made a belly landing.

An improperly aligned vent bracket had enabled smoke and hot rocket exhaust to enter into the aft fuselage, and in addition the combustion chamber had developed a hairline crack. Fuel had leaked out and ignited on the hot outer wall of the combustion chamber, causing several cables to begin smoldering from the heat. This was the first flight of a conventional aircraft using liquid-fueled rocket propulsion. The Heinkel team repaired the airplane, and test flights resumed in June 1937. One of these was a takeoff using both piston and rocket propulsion. That same month Erich Warsitz made a complete flight in the He 112R-V2 exclusively under rocket power, with the piston engine's propeller feathered the entire flight. Takeoff went smoothly; Warsitz pulled into a climb, made a circuit of the field and, when the rocket cut out, drifted back down to land.

This flight very pointedly demonstrated the feasibility of rocket propulsion for aircraft. The main difference between the He 112R and the flights by Stamer, Espenlaub, and von Opel in the late 1920s was not only the use of a liquid-fueled rocket, but also the fact that, with the He 112R, the rocket system was mounted in the tail instead of near the aircraft's center of gravity, as had the solid fueled rockets on the earlier flights.

In the interim, Hellmuth Walther had developed a rocket propulsion system that used hydrogen peroxide (H_2O_2) as the carrier for oxygen and methanol as the fuel. Using a catalytic converter the hydrogen peroxide broke down into steam and oxygen, which was then burned with the methanol. This made it safer than the system developed by Wernher von Braun, which harbored a latent danger of explosion at the moment of ignition due to the possibility of a combustible mix-

ture already existing inside the combustion chamber.

This rocket system was tested in both the He 72 and the Fw 56, plus there were also successful flights using the HWK rocket assisted takeoff units with the He 111 (see the section entitled "Hellmuth Walter Kommaditgesellschaft" in the chapter "Rocket Engines"). It was time for Hellmuth Walter's rocket system to be tested in the He 112R as well. To this end the RLM awarded HWK a contract in 1937 for building a corresponding rocket propulsion system. This system incorporated a pump feed for the fuel, and was thus the direct forerunner of the HKW RI-203, which later came to power the He 176.

Thus, in 1937 there existed two Heinkel He 112Rs at Neuhardenberg: the He 112R-V2,which was fitted with a rocket motor developed by Wernher von Braun and powered by liquid oxygen and ethyl alcohol; and the He 112 R-V3, with its HWK rocket system fueled by hydrogen peroxide and *Z-Stoff* (methanol). Testing of the He 112R-V3 lasted into the fall of 1937, with Erich Warsitz as the test pilot at the controls here as well. It should be mentioned at this point that many sources claim that the He 112R-V3 flew before the first successful flight of the He 112R-V2, but today's evidence makes this claim very difficult to confirm. The V3's performance prompted Ernst Heinkel to develop a special rocket plane that would be designed exclusively for this new medium of propulsion. Together with his colleagues and Erich Warsitz he began examining potential design layouts for this rocket plane. Two options were decided upon: either a small, light and fast machine or a larger, slower, and safer design. Heinkel left the choice to Warsitz, who of course was ultimately the one who would be flying the plane and taking the risk. Warsitz decided on the first option—a small and fast plane—as he felt this would more clearly demonstrate the characteristics of rocket propulsion. This was the theoretical moment of birth for the Heinkel He 176.

With the construction of the Peenemünde rocket test center looming in the background, in late 1937 everything down to the last tent was packed up at Neuhardenberg and carted away. Soon there was nothing left to indicate the pioneering efforts and foundation-laying experiments that had taken place at the airfield.

With the He 176, Heinkel intended to push the speed envelope to 1,000 km/h. This would involve a two-stage plan, as follows:

The He 176-V1 would be equipped with the more reliable Walter RI-203 rocket engine and would be used for flight testing at speeds of up to 700 km/h, whereas the He 176-V2 would be propelled by the more powerful rocket system of Wernher von Braun and tested to speeds up to 1000 km/h.

Wernher von Braun, therefore, after moving from Kummersdorf to Peenemünde East, continued apace at his work on liquid-propelled rocket motors for aircraft. In addition to test bench run-ups, from early 1939 onwards static tests with the engine were conducted with the He 112R-V2. These, however, went quite slowly, as many problems cropped up and needed correcting. In all, 180 burn tests were carried out on the test bench by the middle of May 1939. The engine had been designated the RII-101a in the meantime and delivered a thrust of 1,000 kp with a burn time of 120 seconds. Even with the engine not quite complete, it had reached a certain stage of maturity that it was felt flight trials could be risked.

For this reason the He 112R-V2 was moved to Peenemünde West on 9 June 1939. Erich Warsitz subsequently flew a complete test program of 24 flights that same month. The He 112R-V2 test program was then put to rest for awhile, but in the summer of 1940—despite an RLM ban on the He 176 program—was resumed, and flight testing continued. This was made possible by the fact that the He 112R-V2 program had been taken over by the *Heereswaffenamt*, and that Wernher von Braun belonged to the *Heer* test center at Peenemünde East.

During this continuation of activity, test pilot and engineer Gerhard Reins became increasingly involved in the program in order to give Erich Warsitz some respite. On 18 June 1940 Reins took off in the He 112R-V2 on a speed test flight with and without rocket propulsion. The plane crashed, with fatal consequences for Reins. The reason was a hairline crack in the cooling mantle of the combustion chamber, releasing a fine alcohol/water mixture mist that ignited and damaged the elevator controls. Following this accident, the *Heer*

test center at Peenemünde East ceased all activities involving rocket-powered aircraft, as had the *Luftwaffe* test center at Peenemünde West earlier.

He 176

Based on the favorable results with the Heinkel He 112R, Ernst Heinkel decided to build a special rocket-powered aircraft in the summer of 1937 in order to better investigate and demonstrate the performance handling of rocket motors.

To this end the in-house *Sonderentwicklung II* (Special Developments II) department was established. Design of the aircraft was left with *Ing.* Walter Günter; overseeing development was Heinkel's chief designer, Karl Schwärzler. Others on the development team included Siegfried Günter and Prof. Dr. Hertel, with the latter being responsible for overall design and development of the program. The aircraft was to be laid out for high speeds in level flight and have excellent climb performance. It should be remembered that, at this time, knowledge of aerodynamics in the transonic region was in its infancy. Furthermore, the airplane was to take off and land at subsonic speeds, but at the same time have the capability of approaching the speed of sound—a unique combination of requirements at the time.

After debating on the rocket propulsion system to be used, the decision rested on the system developed by Hellmuth Walter, an engineer in Kiel who had promised a reliable system by the end of 1938. In the meantime, he'd developed a controllable rocket engine running on hydrogen peroxide as an oxidizer and methanol as the fuel. This made it safer than von Braun's design, which continued to have problems with its combustion chamber. Wernher von Braun was not able to promise Heinkel delivery of an engine before 1939—another reason why the Walter engine was selected. As a compromise, Heinkel was forced to acknowledge that the Walter engine only offered 600 kp of thrust, compared to the 1,000 kp of thrust with the Braun rocket system.

In its dimensions the He 176-V1 was tailored precisely to the body weight of Erich Warsitz and the Walter engine. Two prototype aircraft were planned—one for researching flight handling at lower speeds, and a second for high speed regions. This second prototype was to receive the more powerful engine of Wernher von Braun once it had reached operational safety. This never materialized. Development and construction of the He 176-V1 took place at the Heinkel Works in Rostock-Marienehe, in the same hangar as the first jet aircraft in the world, the He 178. Construction of the plane began in the late fall of 1937, and parallel to this there were many questions still needing answers.

At the same time as construction started, testing began with a 1.80 m metal model of the He 176-V1 at the DVL's high speed wind tunnel in Berlin-Adlershof under the direction of Dr. Tietjenz.

For the first time ever, this airplane was to have seam welded wings so that they could be used as integral tanks. Up to then wings had been riveted, and any wing tanks available would be specially adapted to fit into the wing. But welding the hydromalium wings initially posed some problems, and a second wing was built in standard two-spar fashion so as not to jeopardize the He 176-V1's testing timetable.

Because of the aircraft's minimal frontal area the fuselage cross section around the pilot's head was just 70 cm, meaning that he was to fly the plane from a semi-prone position. For this reason it became neces-

sary to develop a special back parachute instead of the common seat parachute normally carried. In order for him to have a good field of view, it was planned to have the entire upper front fuselage incorporate a bubble type streamlined canopy. This bubble canopy, made of acrylic, was to be manufactured as a single piece. A long series of experiments were needed before the canopy's measurements were sufficient to absorb the stress. Prior to this, stress cracks repeatedly appeared in the canopy material. As reinforcement, three stiffener ribs were integrated into the design so that the canopy would have adequate support and not become deformed—something that would lead to optical distortions. Furthermore, the entire upper fuselage (length 1.50 meters) was designed as an escape capsule for safety reasons. It could be separated from the remainder of the fuselage by electrically activated explosive bolts, with a compressed air system using three air cylinders aiding separation. A parachute would retard the fall of the capsule, enabling the pilot to unbuckle himself and take to his own 'chute. Several hundred simulated "rescue shots" were successfully carried out to test this safety measure and prove the functional reliability of the system prior to a wooden mockup of the forward fuselage being used to conduct

This photo, rediscovered a few years ago, reputedly shows the He 176 during taxi trials at Peenemünde. (*Deutsches Museum Munich*)

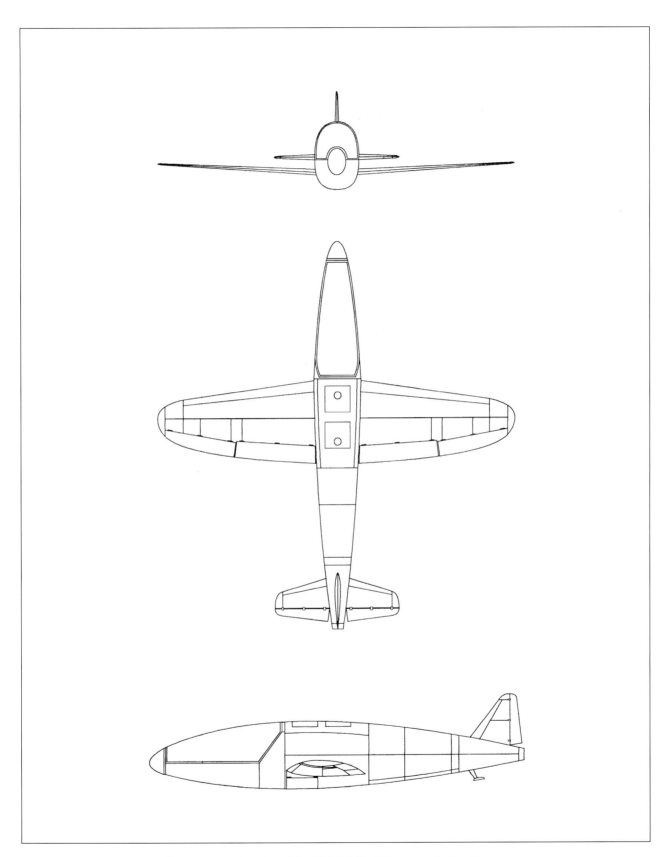

An erroneous drawing of the Heinkel He 176 prepared after the war.

jettison trials. These trials involved the mockup being carried to an altitude of 6,000 to 7,000 meters and dropped from an He 111. As a result, the parachute was equipped with its own extraction system to ensure that it would deploy fully. Finally, a successful test was made with an original forward fuselage section, with a dummy (of the same dimensions as Erich Warsitz) simulating the pilot.

The entire escape method involved an orderly plan that required precise adherence. The pilot initiated separation of the cockpit from the fuselage by means of a lever located to the left above his head. The capsule's aerodynamic shape enabled it to continue forward, whereas the fuselage—now with a blunt forward section—would rapidly decelerate and drop behind. Once the capsule had traveled about 1,000 meters, the pilot would pull a lever to the right above his head and deploy the pod's 'chute, which reduced the descent to about 300 km/h. Now the pilot could release the canopy and bail out. Not until a certain distance separated him from the capsule and after the descent speed of the pilot had slowed to about 175 km/h

(through aerodynamic drag) would the pilot then release his own parachute. The requisite altitude for a safe escape process at a speed of about 1,000 km/h was 6,000 meters. Any lower altitude could not guarantee a safe egress.

The airframe of the Heinkel He 176 was completed in the early summer of 1938.

The factory airfield at Rostock-Marienehe was too small for testing the He 176-V1, so the aircraft and its developmental team under Walter Künzel were moved to Peenemünde. It was transported with wings removed on a special cargo truck under the cover of night. At Peenemünde the Walter RI-203, with its 600 kp static thrust and 60 second burn time, was fitted into the airplane.

First on the program's agenda were static trials using the rocket engine, designed to permit adjustment of operation and throttle control. These brought with them several modifications and changes. At the Peenemünde West site was a technical team from HWK under the direction of *Ing.* Asmus Bartelsen (who had also taken over the management of the HWK team at Neuhardenberg in 1937), which would be re-

---

Technical Configuration:

Role:	single-engined rocket powered test aircraft
Crew:	one pilot
Wings:	cantilever low-wing of all-metal construction. Initially twin spar design, later replaced by an integral "wet wing" constructed of welded hydronalium; virtually elliptical cross section with straight leading edge; sharp straight wing tips; laminar profile; ailerons situated outboard; split flaps located between ailerons and fuselage
Fuselage:	metal alloy monocoque design; symmetrical teardrop shape with slight droop to nose; entire forward fuselage designed as an escape module with integrated pneumatically activated parachute (separates pneumatically from aft fuselage); pilot flies the aircraft from an almost prone position
Empennage:	standard cantilever design of all-metal construction
Undercarriage:	pneumatically retractable main gear with fixed tail skid; 0.8 m wheel track
Engine:	1 x HWK RI 203 offering 600 kp static thrust, located in center fuselage section; combustion chamber in aft fuselage section; tank system made of pure aluminum to accommodate hydrogen peroxide (320 liters = 430 kg) and methanol (22 liters = 33 kg) between the fuselage break bulkhead and the rocket engine, as well as additional hydrogen peroxide tanks in each wing (2 x 20 liters = 60 kg); pump fed hydrogen peroxide and pressurized air fed methanol fuel systems
Military equipment:	none

sponsible for the technical side of the engine test program. By the fall of 1938 the rocket engine had reached a level of reliability where it was felt that tow trials could begin along the beach at Usedom. One of the most powerful vehicles of the day, a 7.6 liter Mercedes compressor truck, was used to tow the He 176-V1. But the 155 km/h speed it clocked was inadequate for satisfactorily assessing the airplane's control and roll characteristics. Warsitz therefore decided to carry out the roll tests by using the rocket motor, which could only briefly be powered on for this purpose. Time limitations could be made by adjusting the quantity of fuel. Any other type of control was not possible, as the engine was either at full thrust or zero thrust; there was no middle stage. The real problem here was with the stabilizers, which had been designed for speeds of around 800 km/h and would have little effect at the significantly lesser liftoff (rotation) speeds. This ultimately would result in severe limitations on the directional stability in this situation. This meant that steering on the ground could only be accomplished by unilateral application of the brakes, something that was not entirely without its dangers given the narrow tracked undercarriage of the He 176-V1. In addition, the airfield's grass strip had to be cleared of "new" molehills prior to any flight, since these could easily cause the plane to veer uncontrollably. This quite often might end in a ground loop, for the wing tips were just 60 centimeters above the ground. During the testing, there was constantly a large stockpile of canopies and wingtips kept on hand at Peenemünde. They even went so far as to build a kind of "rollbar" (lateral skids on the wings) for the aircraft. Erich Warsitz gradually increased the taxi speed until the aircraft just cleared the ground. As soon as the plane was back down, it was necessary to brake immediately to avoid overshooting the 1,200 meter long runway with the He 176-V1. The winter of 1938/39 was used for carrying out a number of changes and improvements on the airplane and the rocket motor, including attaching the now-finished welded wings to the aircraft. Taxi trials resumed in March 1939, and the first proper hops to altitudes of 2-5 meters were conducted. From March to May Warsitz flew more than 100 brief flights (over a maximum flight distance of 100 meters) at varying altitudes (up to 20 meters)

On 20 June 1939 it was finally time. Erich Warsitz had just made the first flight in the He 1760V1.

On the occasion of a celebration on 15 September 1959, the 20th anniversary of the maiden flights of the He 176-V1 and He 178, Warsitz described the event in detail:

"…Once I thought I was familiar with the plane's quirks and features after having done endless taxi runs at ever increasing speeds, I suddenly decided to make the first real flight late in the evening of 20 June 1939. I refused to be deterred by all the engineers and mechanics who wanted to make a detailed inspection of the engine and the airframe beforehand.

"Because of my sudden decision, I had no time to inform Heinkel—although he had given strict instructions to do so. He didn't think badly of me later when I told him the news of my success.

"After my decision to fly the plane immediately, all the engineers and mechanics became eerily quiet. No one spoke a word; everyone knew that they were facing a moment in time that would decide the future. With feverish energy the machine was fueled and made ready for the flight. I put on my parachute myself, took Künzel, the directing engineer, to one side, and asked him to pass on a letter in my writing desk if anything were to happen to me.

"…The machine was towed to the starting point. I climbed in, checked all the switches, control surfaces and instruments, pressurized the tanks, then got the sign that the runway was OK. Künzel came over and, without a sound, shook my hand. The crewmen closed the canopy, and I then gave it full throttle.

"I was used to the unusual acceleration force which built up even during the roll. But because of the tanks, which had been filled to capacity for the first time, I needed a longer takeoff roll. At around 300 km/h, just before lifting off, the left wing caught the ground. The airplane, which up to that point I had only been able to keep straight using the brake pedals, swerved to the left, and I saw a disaster brewing. However, by hook and crook I poured on the gas, and shortly thereafter it lifted off, slipping to the side and oscillating wildly. Speed increased dramatically from 500 km/h to 750 km/h after takeoff. Acceleration was now so great that my head was pushed against the backrest. A slight movement on the stick and the bird shot into the skies at a 45° angle without a drop in speed, which gave me a healthy respect for the plane. However, I had to make a left banking turn immediately, a very steep one indeed, otherwise I'd get too far away from the field, and the fuel only lasted for a minute. Everything went wonderfully, and it was an uplifting feeling for me to fly around the tip of Usedom at 800 km/h in virtual silence. I didn't have time for flight tests, as it was already time to focus on the landing. Again I succeeded in making a sharp left turn to set up for the approach, when the engine shut down just as I was making the descent—the tanks were empty. I was noticeably thrown forward into the harness by the deceleration caused by the air's braking effect. I pushed the stick, whisked over the Peene, and headed for the ground at a speed of 500 km/h. Reaching the edge of the runway, the airplane bounced several times, then rolled to a stop."

The following day, 21 June 1939, the aircraft was demonstrated before Ernst Heinkel, *Generalluftzeugmeister* Ernst Udet, Erhard Milch, and other representatives from the RLM. Everyone present was visibly impressed with the flying qualities of the little He 176-V1. Nevertheless, Udet forbade any further work on this "rocket with running-boards," as he called the airplane. One of the reasons for this may well have been his concern for Erich Warsitz who, as a Rechlin test pilot, belonged as always to the RLM, and whose life he didn't want to unnecessarily risk. In the end, Heinkel and Warsitz were able to at least convince Udet to allow Heinkel to continue work on the He 176-V1 at his own expense.

With regard to the test program and the He 176-V1's performance before the RLM's representatives, there have been several conflicting reports in publications. For example, we can read that an unofficial first flight took place as early as 15 June 1939, with a demonstration of the He 176-V1 for RLM representatives four weeks even before that. These discrepancies may have their basis in the fact that no original documents relating to the He 176-V1 now exist, and the investigation of these various authors rely upon the memories of those involved which, however, could only be put to paper after the war.

On 3 July 1939 Hitler was given a demonstration of several new airplanes produced by Germany's aviation industry at Rechlin. The He 176-V1 was also shown to Adolf Hitler on this day at the Rogentin airfield, a satellite of Rechlin about 3 kilometers distant. But here too, Hitler, Göring, Keitel, Milch, Jodl, and Udet showed little interest in the He 176. Göring even went so far as to call the He 176-V1 a "nice little toy."

Even a discussion a few days later in berlin between Erich Warsitz, Hitler, and Göring changed nothing with regard to the RLM's opinion of the rocket plane. Ernst Heinkel at least was given permission to continue the project at his own expense. Further testing of the He 176-V1 was therefore transferred from Peenemünde back to Rostock-Marienehe, where Warsitz carried out a few more test flights. One of these even saw him reaching a speed of 850 km/h at full burn of the rocket engine.

The He 176-V1 had by now been worn out from a flying standpoint, and the more powerful rocket engine of Wernher von Braun would not fit into the V1's airframe since, because of the many changes required, it would not have been able to withstand the higher speeds without much difficulty. For this reason Heinkel had the He 176-V2 under construction, although this never flew, because shortly after the outbreak of the Second World War the Heinkel He 176 abruptly came to a halt. On 12 September 1939 Udet ordered "the reduction of developmental plans in favor of necessary concentration." This list included a total of 31 points, and at position 29 it read specifically "He 176—all work to be stopped immediately."

For a long time the airplane lounged in a hangar at the Rostock-Marienehe Works. It was eventually disassembled and shipped to Berlin's Aviation Museum (at the Lehrter Station) in sealed crates where, still packed in its crates, it was destroyed in a bombing raid in 1944.

By the time the war ended, the experience gained with the Heinkel He 176 had flowed directly into Heinkel's *Julia* rocket fighter project.

He P.1077 "*Julia*"

Because of the ever increasing number of enemy bomber formations penetrating the skies of Germany, by the spring of 1944 the RLM's clamor for a disposable fighter grew increasingly louder. After a successful attack the pilot was expected to separate from the enemy and then bail out. An actual landing was to take place only in extreme emergencies.

A direct result of this requirement began in the early summer of 1944 within Heinkel's Vienna project bureau under the direction of Dr. Gerloff. The team initiated conceptual studies involving a hybrid mixture of a manned anti-aircraft missile and a simplified high speed miniature rocket-propelled fighter. The project carried the internal Heinkel project number P.1077 and was given the covername *Julia*.

The first type sheet on this aircraft was submitted for review on 16 June 1944. It was to be a high wing design with a circular fuselage cross section. The design revealed a twin rudder configuration with rectangular vertical stabilizers. The pilot was housed in a prone position inside the cockpit. Planned propulsion was provided by a rocket system with separate climb and cruise combustion chambers, with two additional solid fuel rockets used to accelerate during takeoff attached to the side of the fuselage. Armament was to have been two MG 151/20 in pods beneath the wings. Deviating from the requirement were two landing skids in tandem. In early September 1944 the RLM studied all designs submitted to the "disposable plane" requirement. As is known, the Bachem *Natter* emerged the victor from this contest. But the Heinkel *Julia* also had its supporters, so that a contract for 20 prototypes was also issued to the Vienna Heinkel Works. These aircraft were to be manufactured exclusively of wood on standardized production tables.

Following this decision Heinkel worked feverishly on a final design description, that was ultimately submitted to the RLM in mid-October 1944. This included various subvariants of the *Julia*:

1. non-powered trainer version with prone pilot and 2 x MG 151/20 armament in pods
2. pre-production as before, but with an HWK rocket system and for solid fuel RATO packs
3. as before, but the 2 x MG 151/20 pod armament swapped out for 2 x MK 108 cannons integrated into either side on the fuselage
4. as before, but with pilot seated and raised canopy
5. as #4, but a ramjet engine on the fuselage spine in place of the rocket system. Takeoff was planned via catapult or 2/4 solid fuel RATO rockets. This variant was designated *Romeo*.

In a meeting on 26 October 1944 between Heinkel and his leading colleagues it was decided that the pilot would be seated in the cockpit in all versions. Furthermore, for production simplification the wings would be of a simple rectangular shape. In addition, the dual rudders were replaced by a simple central rudder, and a central landing skid replaced the two skids formerly planned. The fuselage height was increased by 10 centimeters to boost the fuel capacity. Planned armament would now be 2 x MK 108 cannons, each with 40 rounds, one on either side of the pilot's seat. Unguided R4M rockets in jettisonable packs beneath each wing was also an option.

In October models in 1/20 scale were built for the first free flight tests, and by the end of that month an additional model of the *Julia* in 1/8 scale with central and dual rudders was available.

He 176-V2 Project Data

empty weight:	400 kg
fuel:	500 kg
takeoff weight:	1000 kg
max thrust:	1000 kp
min thrust:	300 kp
wing loading (takeoff):	200 kg/m^2
wing loading (landing):	100 kg/m^2
wing area:	5 m^2
wingspan:	5 m
length:	approx. 6 m
max fuselage diameter:	approx. 0.7 m
max speed:	1000 km/h
min speed:	179 km/h
average climb rate:	67 m/s
time to 10,000 m:	2.5 minutes
engine:	liquid-fuel rocket engine using liquid oxygen/alchohol fuel combination

A bombing raid on the Vienna Heinkel Works destroyed all plans for the *Julia*. The RLM held a crisis meeting, during the course of which the requirement was issued for a test type (by this was probably meant a wooden mockup of the aircraft in 1/1 scale) to be made available by mid-November 1944. Heinkel submitted a reworked type description of the *Julia* dated 16 November 1944. Almost at the same time a corresponding contract for construction was issued by the Heinkel Works to the Niemitz & Son Cabinetmakers in Klosterneuburg, which had already done mockup work for Messerchmitt, and thus had the necessary experience.

One important stipulation of this description of 16 November 1944 was that any influence from the He 162 program must be avoided.

The airplane was laid out with a standard tail to avoid taking any unnecessary developmental risks, obtain good flight handling qualities, and be able to present a finished product as quickly as possible. With regard to armament and engine the aircraft configuration was to be kept as flexible as possible in order to incorporate up-to-date experience in these areas. The airplane was expected to reach speeds that would be markedly higher than the Allied escort fighters, on the one hand to make penetration of fighter defenses easier, and on the other to ensure a safe escape from the enemy following a successful attack.

A significant problem for rocket-powered planes is their limited range and the sharply restricted effective operational area this entailed. Therefore, the tank capacity of the aircraft was designed so that once the enemy was found, two or three attack runs and a safe escape from the enemy were possible. In doing so, it should be remembered that a single rocket-powered takeoff burned about 40% of the fuel alone. For economic reasons it became necessary to calculate the fuel quantity so that more than one attack was possible, while at the same time ensuring that the increased fuel weight or larger aircraft dimensions did not negatively impact the airplane's flight handling. Nevertheless, the *Julia* was conceived with a view toward the greatest possible savings in weight, and with regard for the simplest production methods. Among other things, the weight distribution made this clear.

The goal was to make possible production of the individual components themselves in small factories, or even as a cottage industry using the simplest of jigs and machinery. Underlying this was the fact that production of the *Julia* could not impact other aircraft types.

The type description spelled out the aircraft's role as follows: "daylight engagement of bomber formations," as well as point defense and air superiority over critical areas of the front lines. The requirement was also that, for camouflage reasons and for independent operations, there would be no fixed airfields. At the same time, massed formation takeoffs were to be possible, since the short flight time of rocket-powered aircraft prohibited the normal forming up in a specific area prior to attacking. Because of the simple design of the plane, each point in the combat arena was to be flown visually or with the aid of simple instrumentation, based on anti-aircraft direction methods. The com-

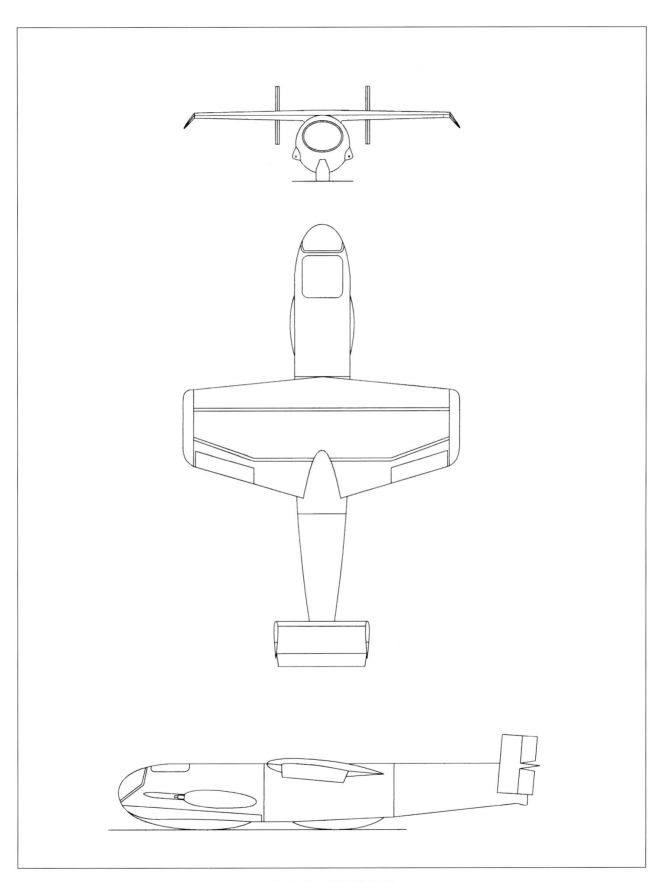

Heinkel P.1077 "*Julia I*"

Heinkel P.1077 *Julia* Weight Table

Crew:	90 kg
Armament and ammunition:	182 kg
Armor:	61 kg
Other equipment:	20 kg
Military payload = 353 kg	
Airframe	380 kg
Rocket (incl. 10 kg fuel)	180 kg
Tanks:	32 kg
C-Stoff:	200 kg
T-Stoff:	650 kg
Takeoff weight (minus booster rockets):	= 1,795 kg
Takeoff weight (with booster rockets):	2,275 kg

plicated fighter direction method was to be avoided at all costs. These additional requirements favored either a vertical takeoff or steep angle takeoff followed by a steep climb.

By the war's end a few model tests of the vertical takeoff method had been carried out using a platform frame to be developed in-house. Because of the extra time involved in developing this platform frame to production standards the first aircraft would be launched by standard horizontal takeoff procedures.

As this type description reflects, Heinkel had distanced itself from the idea of a pure disposable fighter. Heinkel saw that the greater danger was that the pilot, suspended in his 'chute after bailing out, was a ripe target for enemy aircraft. The airplane thus was fitted with a landing skid so that after a successful attack the airplane could be brought in for a landing. Furthermore, the pilot on his "bench" could extricate himself from the plane in case a bailout proved necessary, even at higher speeds. At the same time, a prerequisite was that the takeoff method used would need to be kept simple, both from a technical as well as a fly-

ing standpoint, in order to keep the pilot training requirements to a minimum.

One expression of the Heinkel philosophy regarding fighter construction is revealed in this design. The human factor was not forgotten in all the requirements made, as well as the peripheral stipulations. On the one hand, this was made evident by the minimal training demands the company was striving for, and on the other hand it was manifest quite clearly in the planned means of escape for the pilot. A view that carried through all fighter designs produced by Heinkel.

Planned completion date for the first flight-ready aircraft was to have been the 24 January 1945. Since, however, large scale production of the He 162 consumed the entire production capacity of the Vienna Heinkel Works, delays on construction of the *Julia* were inevitable. Therefore, on 5 February 1945 the RLM relayed instructions to Director Franke at Heinkel to immediately cease any further work on the *Julia*. The instructions, however, were not passed on, and work continued on the project in an unofficial capacity. In March 1945, at the instigation of *Ing.* Lusser,

Technical Configuration:

Role:	single-jet point defense fighter
Crew:	one pilot
Wings:	cantilever mid-wing made of wood. Wings based on He 162 wings, no flaps, 5 degree sweepback
Fuselage:	made of wood. Pilot in prone position in pressurized cockpit with entry hatch above the cockpit
Empennage:	twin rudders capping the horizontal stabilizers, made of wood, located above combustion chamber at the extreme aft end of the fuselage
Undercarriage:	single center landing skid beneath the fuselage
Engine:	1 x HWK 109-509 A-2 with 200 - 1,700 kp thrust and auxiliary cruise combustion chamber of 150- 300 kp thrust, *C-Stoff* tank in cockpit above pilot, *T-Stoff* tank located between cockpit/ fuselage and engine bulkheads
Military Equipment:	2 x MK 108 machine cannons incorporated into either side of fuselage

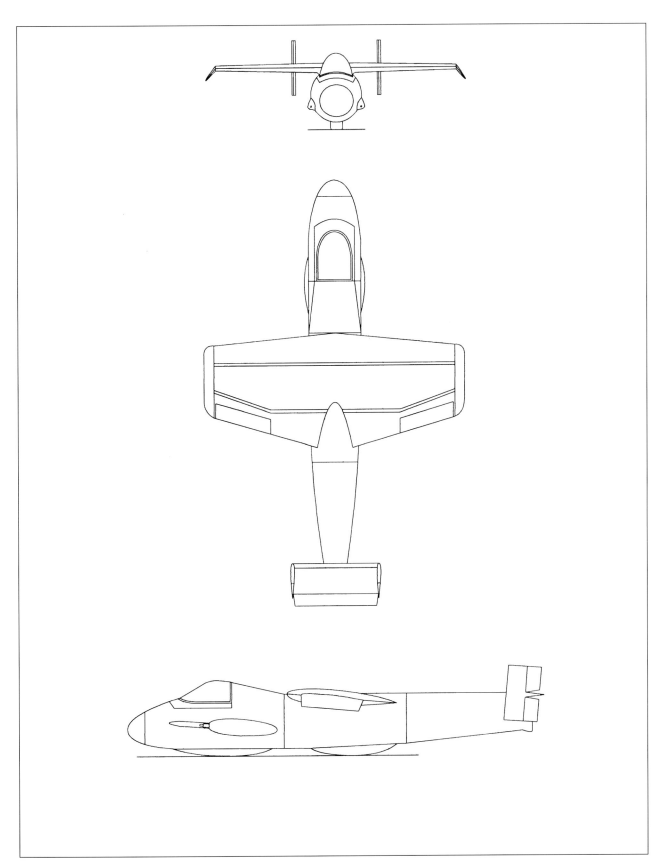

Heinkel P.1077 "*Julia II*"

work was officially authorized to resume, and two non-powered and two powered prototypes were to be constructed.

By the end of the war several prototypes were said to have been built in addition to a full-scale mockup, although whether any of these took to the air cannot be determined with any degree of certainty. Given the situation and the circumstances in the last days of the war, it is highly unlikely that any flight ever took place.

In early April Soviet troops occupied Neuhaus on the Triesting, the center of *Julia* development; they reputedly acquired numerous blueprints and documents. The mockup and the prototypes, however, had been destroyed by Heinkel employees.

Parallel to this *Julia* design in early 1945 was a second design in the works, the *Julia II*, at the Heinkel plant in Vienna. This was based on variant 4 from October 1944. The main difference here was that the pilot was housed in the upright, seated position within the cockpit, and had an all-view canopy resting on a strengthened fuselage. Because of the larger fuselage cross section, this variant had slightly poorer performance figures than the *Julia I*, as has been described earlier.

Since rocket engines remained ticklish and dangerous affairs at this date—demonstrated by the many non-combat losses suffered by the Me 163—Heinkel looked into an alternative to the *Julia*. They made use of the *Julia II*'s airframe and mated it with a Schmidt-Argus ramjet having a thrust of 750 kp in place of the rocket engine. This design was called the *Romeo I*, and although it did not achieve the estimated flight performance of a *Julia II*, it did have a much greater range. A *Romeo II* derived from the *Romeo I*, which had a larger wingspan, with a goal of achieving a lower wing loading due to the lesser thrust.

Neither *Romeo* design was ever built, however—victims of a lack of production capacity at Heinkel and a shortage of ramjets at the Argus company.

Messerschmitt

The Long Road to the Messerschmitt Me 163 *Komet*
The Me 163's history stretches far into the distant past, to the '20s of the previous century. After Alexander Lippisch assumed technical directorship of the *Rhön-Rossiten Gesellschaft* on the Wasserkuppe in 1925 he began designing gliders and sailplanes. These designs he infused with his most primal interest, the tailless configuration.

At first Lippisch drew up sailplanes for the *Storch* series. Lippisch's *Storch I* flew for the first time as early as 1927. Sailplane trials were completed in 1929 under the direction of pilot Günter Groenhoff. The aircraft was then fitted with an 8 hp DKW engine, giving it a speed of 125 km/h at a weight of 125 kg. Nevertheless, these efforts met with little favorable reception at the RLM. One party who was interested, however, was the Atlantic-crossing pilot Hermann Köhl, who wanted the *Rhön-Rossiten Gesellschaft* to build him a sailplane. Although the plane crashed during a demonstration by Günter Groenhoff at the Böllenfalltor satellite airfield near Darmstadt, Köhl transferred 4,200 *Reichsmark* to Lippisch for construction of the *Delta I*. The *Delta I* was powered by a 30 hp Bristol Cherup engine, which gave it a top speed of 145 km/h. The *Delta* series was the first aircraft to incorporate a tailless low wing design, a "flying wing." The *Delta I* was

of a cantilever delta wing configuration with rudders capping the wing tips. The all-wooden airplane had a two-seat cockpit and was fitted with a pusher propeller. Its first flight as a glider took place in the summer of 1930, with powered flight first occurring in May 1931. In October 1931 Lippisch once again made the attempt, and Goenhoff flew the *Delta I* in a demonstration for the *Verkehrsministerium*, but yet again little interest was shown.

After a tiresome search for funding, the next project was the *Delta III*, whose construction would be undertaken by Focke-Wulf. At the same time Gerhard Fieseler showed an interest in the concept, and with this as a basis he had the Fieseler F3 *Wespe* designed and built. But Fieseler had flown the airplane without Lippisch's permission and crashed it, subsequently losing interest in the idea.

Because of poor longitudinal stability, Lippisch's flying wing design was considered difficult to fly in flying circles, and it was only thanks to the flying abilities of a certain Günter Groenhoff that the project had advanced as far as it did. But on 23 July 1932 Groenhoff was fatally injured in a crash at the Rhön Competition, ushering in a difficult period of time for Alexander Lippisch. As 1933 turned into 1934 the RRG moved to Darmstadt-Griesheim and became a

Steps on the Path to the Me 163:	
Storch I	flying wing glider, completed in 1927 at the RRG
Storch II	smaller version of Storch I
Storch III	follow-on development of Storch I to two-seat glider, first flight 1928
Storch IV	two-seat powered sailplane, built 1928
Storch V	sailplane, tested 1929
Delta I	
Delta II	follow-on development of Delta I
Delta III	built in 1934 at Focke Wulf; crashed in 1935, killing pilot Wiegmeier
Delta IV	built in 1934 Fieseler as a twin-engine acft, crashed during testing
Delta IVb	rebuilt and modified Delta IV at DFS
DFS 39	follow-on development of Delta IVb with 75 hp engine
Delta IVc	follow-on development of the DFS 39 as a two-seat sportplane

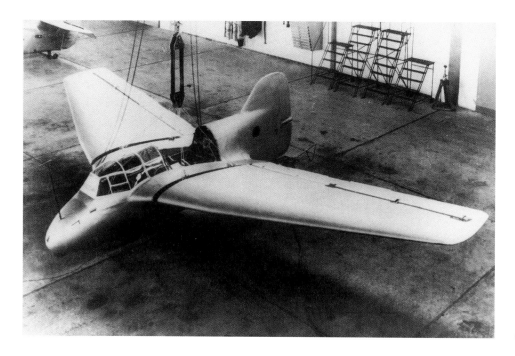

The DFS 194 in the assembly hangar. The wing separation joint can clearly be seen here.

part of the DFS. From that point on, Lippisch focused exclusively on his *Delta III* and *Delta IV* flying wing projects. But the most difficult problem was the shortage of qualified test pilots. Hans Deutschmann crashed while attempting a takeoff. Hubert damaged the *Delta III* during a post-maintenance check flight, and Wiegmeier crashed both the *Delta III* and the *Delta IV* within the space of just a few days. As a result the RLM wanted to cancel the DFS' flying wing projects, and it was only thanks to the incessant efforts of Pro-

fessor Georgii, the director of the DFS, that the RLM not only backed away from its position, but also put up additional funding for construction of further *Delta IV* aircraft. This was the moment of birth for the *Delta IVc*, which would also be known as the DFS 39.

Heini Dittmar (chief test pilot for the DFS from 1939 onward) was the first to master the *Delta* aircraft in the air, so that the *Delta IVc* was even given an airworthiness certification as a two seat sportplane with a 75 hp Pobjoy engine, even if it never went into production.

Delta IVc Characteristics:
- cantiliver tailless low wing design
- downward canted wingtips
- rudders as wingtip caps
- pronounced 20 degree wing sweepback
- elevators on wing trailing edges
- composite construction with wooden wings
- shrouded single-strut shock-absorbed undercarriage legs and tail skid
- two-seat
- piston engine driving tractor propeller in the nose
- civil registration as sportplane (D-ENFL)
- Technical Data:

wingspan:	9.60 m
length:	5.40 m
empty weight:	390 kg
takeoff weight:	600 kg
maximum speed:	200 km/h

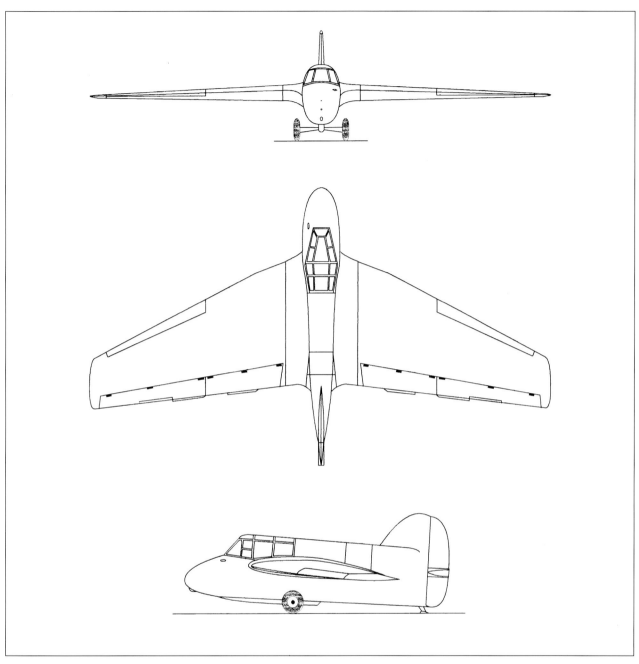

DFS 194

DFS 194 and Project X

In 1936 Hellmuth Walter provided the DVL with his rocket propulsion system, which offered 135 kp of thrust for a period of 45 seconds. Dr. A. Baeumker at the RLM's research department latched on to the idea of rocket propulsion for a small high performance airplane. Via his colleague Dr. Lorenz, in 1937 he contracted with Alexander Lippisch at the DFS to design a special airframe based on the results from the DFS 39 and DFS 40. It was to be laid out with an eye toward this new propulsion system. Parallel to this,

Hellmuth Walter received a contract to develop a more powerful rocket engine (300 kp thrust) for this experimental plane.

Both the DFS 39 and the DFS 40 had demonstrated good flight handling and excellent stability in wind tunnel tests at the AVA Göttingen and in free flight trials. The new plane was carried under the designation "Project X," and was kept under the strictest secrecy. At the same time, work continued apace at the DFS on the DFS 194, contracted for in 1935 and designed for piston propulsion with a pusher propeller in the tail.

DFS 194
(photos: Radinger)

**DFS 194 with rocket engine
ignited.**

DFS 194

**DFS 194 - the tiny orifice
for the rocket in the tail is
clearly visible.**

The DFS 194's engine is ignited for the rocket-powered takeoff.

Heini Dittmar standing in front of the DFS 194.

The DFS 194 taking off under rocket power.

For Project X, the fuselage of the DFS 39 would be modified as necessary to accommodate the rocket system, but the wings would be left untouched in view of the fact that they had already proven themselves. In spite of this, the wings would nevertheless need to be aerodynamically adapted to the anticipated higher speeds. Subsequent wind tunnel testing led to dispensing with the dihedral of the DFS 39's wings and incorporating a single, central rudder into the design, as the earlier wingtip rudders had a tendency to flutter at higher speeds. As before, the elevators would remain located along the wing trailing edge. The landing gear was also replaced by a skid. As with the DFS 39, the two part wing was to be built of wood, with construction taking place at DFS itself. However, because of the rocket engine and its aggressive fuel, the fuselage was to be made of metal (lattice frame construction with metal skinning). This was contracted for with the Heinkel company. It soon became apparent, though, that the DFS would be unable to build the aircraft due to capacity constraints. For this reason Alexander Lippisch and 12 of his colleagues moved to the Messerschmitt company at Augsburg-Haunstetten on 2 January 1939, and on this day the company established Department L.

Work continued at Messerschmitt until the war broke out, but was stymied on 2 September 1939 when the program's priority rating was lowered. Although the effects of this were reduced somewhat by shifting project management from the RLM's research branch to its development branch, the latter was nevertheless unable to prevent the cessation of any further work in February 1940. Hitler had directly ordered that all new armament plans were to be halted, since the war was expected to be over with shortly. Lippisch was not satisfied with this and decided to modify the DFS 194, which he had brought with him to Messerschmitt, to take the Walter RI-203 rocket motor (reduced to 400 kp of thrust). The DFS 194 was a good choice for this, as it had a metal fuselage. However, the aircraft was only designed for speeds of around 300 km/h. The DFS 194 V1 was modified accordingly, but the DFS 194 V2 was left unchanged as a glider in order to test the aerodynamics.

Once the DFS 194 V1's airframe was ready, the plane was transported to Peenemünde-Karlshagen, where it was to be mated with the rocket engine. But it was not until mid-1940 that the HWK RI-203 had advanced to the point where it could be integrated into an airframe and be ground tested. In August 1940 the DFS 194 lifted off on its first rocket-powered flight, with pilot Heini Dittmar at the controls. By the end of 1941 he had flown a total of 45 flights under rocket power, reaching speeds of 550 km/h and demonstrating enormous climb rates to altitudes of 3,000 meters.

Me 163 A

The outstanding results of the DFS 194 trials prompted the RLM to take a renewed interest in the program, and authorized that work be continued in conjunction with an increase in the program's priority. And when Hellmuth Walter announced the construction of a more powerful RII-203 engine with 750 kp of thrust, work began in earnest on the design of a high speed airplane, the Me 163 A, that would be a direct descendent of the DFS 194. By February 1941 the Me 163 V4 had

---

Me 163A Design Description

Role:	rocket-powered tailless experimental airplane
Crew:	one pilot
Wings:	cantilever mid-wing made of wood, with plywood skinning, two section, twin spar, tapered with 23.5 degree leading edge sweepback, fixed lift-inducing slats, hydraulically activated underwing landing flaps
Fuselage:	all-metal monocoque made of magnesium alloy, oval fuselage cross section; all blending between fuselage and wings and rudder by aerodynamic plating; entry via starboard opening cockpit canopy; special suit for pilot to include overshoes, helmet and parachute pack
Empennage:	fabric-covered combination elevators and ailerons (elevons) on outer wing trailing edge, central vertical stabilizer made of wood, with tailfin covered in plywood and rudder in fabric
Undercarriage:	jettisonable wheels; central shock absorbed landing skid, extending and retracting pneumatically; skid
Engine:	HWK RII-203 with a controllable thrust of 100 - 750 kp *T-Stoff* tanks in fuselage and *C-Stoff* tanks in the wings
Military equipment:	none

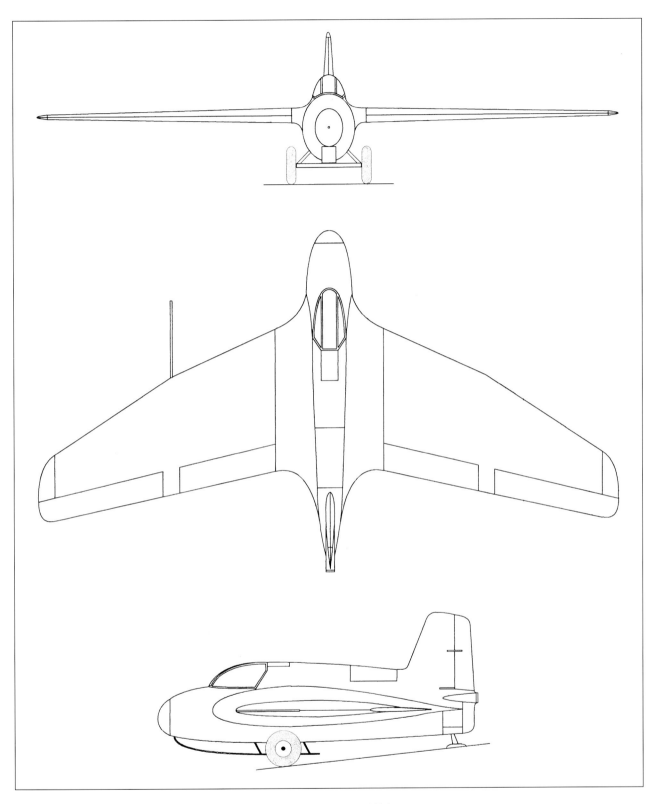

Messerschmitt Me 163 A

been completed at Augsburg as the first of an initial batch of three test prototypes. With this first aircraft, though, there were some problems with the adhesion of the plywood layers along the wing leading edge and the sealing of the main tank in the center wing section.

For reasons of security the RLM selected the designation of Me 163 for this airplane. Originally, the Me 163 was a competitor of the Fieseler Fi 156 *Storch*, and three were built to the requirements for a liaison aircraft. The RLM's view was, however, that it was useful to use the same appellation again, as this would engender no interest whatsoever on the part of the Allies. Thus, the first prototype of the Me 163 A rocket plane was designated the Me 163 A V4.

On 13 February 1941 the Me 163 V4 (KE+SW) was towed behind a Bf 161 V2 from Augsburg-Haunstetten to Lagerlechfeld. There a comprehensive test program began into the flight handling of the unpowered plane, with speeds reaching up to a maximum of 350 km/h. These were achieved by having an Me 110 tow the Me 163 to altitude and releasing it. The smaller plane would then glide back down to the airfield. From the outset, it was apparent that the Me

163 V4 possessed excellent flight handling characteristics, a reflection on the quality of its layout. The Me 163 V4 was subsequently returned to Augsburg-Haunstetten to conduct high speed trials (still without an engine). By increasing the glide angle the speed was also increased incrementally. These tests showed that, at speeds above 360 km/h the ailerons began to flutter; likewise the rudder at about 540 km/h, both of which were corrected by adjusting the counterbalance on the control surfaces. Problems with the different centers of gravity were also fixed at the same time. During the course of this test program Heini Dittmar pushed the Me 163 A to an incredible (for the time) speed of 950 km/h in a dive. Heini Dittmar confirmed the Me 163 A's outstanding glide characteristics, although landings were not always an easy matter.

During an unannounced visit by *Generallluftzeugmeister* Udet at Augsburg, it happened that Dittmar was just completing a test flight in the Me 163 A V4 over the airfield, and Udet followed it with interest. When someone answered a question of his by affirming that this airplane was indeed unpowered, he absolutely refused to believe it in light of the maneuver Dittmar was performing. It wasn't until after the land-

Messerschmitt Me 163 A-VH

ing and a personal inspection of the tiny plane convinced him that no engine was in fact fitted that he accepted the previous answer. This demonstration so impressed Udet that he increased the number of contracted prototypes to 10 and asked Alexander Lippisch to design an operational military version of the Me 163 A. Udet had recognized the advantages of using such a plane for point defense.

In May 1941 the Walter Works received a wooden model of the Me 163 A to make the later integration of the RII-203 rocket engine a smoother process.

But the Walter engines were not available until July 1941, about six months after the planned deadline. To fit the engine, the Me 163 A V4 was towed to Peenemünde. A layover at Rechlin gave pilots Paul Bader and Heinrich Beauvais the opportunity to fly the Me 163 A as a glider. Both confirmed Dittmar's verdict on the excellent flying qualities of the Me 163 A.

After its arrival at Peenemünde West the V4 was fitted with the 750 kp HWK RII-203 rocket engine, and on 18 July 1941 the first test run took place with the installed system. There followed a handful of towed flights with full fuel tanks (filled with water) behind an Me 110 for the intended purpose of evaluating the flight handling of the now heavier airplane. As before, the aircraft behaved quite well, but the increased weight necessitated a higher landing speed at 200 km/h. The first rocket-powered takeoff of the Me 163 A V4 occurred on 13 August 1941 at Karlshagen with Heini Dittmar, the senior test pilot of the Me 163 program, at the controls. Only a limited amount of fuel was carried onboard for this first flight, just enough for the takeoff and an airfield circuit. Over the coming days Dittmar boosted the speed on each flight by carrying an increased quantity of fuel, enabling the engine to burn longer. Speed was measured by cine-theodolites positioned along the beach at Peenemünde. Around this time Rudolf Opitz was also assigned to Peenemünde as the second test pilot. He carried out the third flight of the V4, during which he forgot to jettison the takeoff trolley. He did not notice his mistake until he was at an altitude of 30 meters, by which time it was too late. But thanks to his considerable experience with the DFS 230 transport glider he was able to make a smooth landing with the trolley still in place. By the fourth flight in the Me 163 A Dittmar broke the world speed record of 755 km/h set by Fritz Wendel in 1939 with the Me 209. Yet even then the rocket engine's burn time of 4.5 minutes was not enough for the plane to reach its maximum potential speed after climbing to 3,000 meters. The engine shut off at a speed of 920 km/h when its fuel ran out. On 2 October 1941 Heini Dittmar therefore decided to have his Me 163 A V4 towed behind a Bf 161 to an altitude of 4,000 meters and then ignite the rocket. Even then, the Me 163 A V4 was only 75% filled with fuel.

Heini Dittmar watched in his cockpit as the speedometer climbed above the magic 1,000 km/h mark, but then noticed he was having compressibility problems, and the aircraft bunted over into a steep dive. The plane plunged downward, out of control. Dittmar switched

		Me 163A Experimental Types		
Protype No.	Factory No. (*WerkNr.*)	Identification	Comments
Me 163A V4	163 000 0001	KE+SW	unofficial world record on 2 October 1941 at 1,003.67 km/h
Me 163A V5	163 000 0002	GG+EA	
Me 163A V6	163 000 0003	CD+IK	
Me 163A V7	163 000 0004	CD+IL	ditched in the Baltic Sea in January 1943 due to engine failure
Me 163A V8	163 000 0005	CD+IM	served for a time as testbed for jet rudder; fatal crash of Joschi Pöhs on 30 December 1943
Me 163A V9	163 000 0006	CD+IN	
Me 163A V10	163 000 0007	CD+IO	
Me 163A V11	163 000 0008	CD+IP	
Me 163A V12	163 000 0009	CD+IQ	no engine fitted
Me 163A V13	163 000 0010		no engine fitted

the engine off, and in so doing he was finally able to pull out of the dive. This was the first time ever that an aircraft in level flight had experienced this effect (harbinger of the sound barrier). Later examination of the theodolites showed a speed of 1,003.67 km/h, which equated to Mach 0.84 at that altitude. This was the first flight above 1,000 km/h in the world. For security reasons, though, the record was never made public. By the end of 1941 Dittmar had made a total of 28 flights at full throttle in the V4, at one time achieving a maximum climb rate of 70 meters per second. When it was ferried in on 8 November 1941 the Me 163 A V5 also became available for the testing program. The V5 had larger ailerons—a direct result of previous trials. Like its predecessor, the V5 was first tested as a glider *sans* engine.

Problems continued to plague the Walter engine, particularly with regard to thrust control and aerial restarting. The general problem with thrust control could be solved by an improved manufacturing process of the catalytic converter components. But as before, the engine would often suffer from bucking after being restarted in the air, and reacted quite slowly to the pilot's change in thrust. Furthermore, the engine frequently had a tendency to shut off completely when decelerating. This was a problem that could not even be resolved with the later Me 163B.

On 29 April 1942 the V5, too, was fitted with an engine, thus giving the V4 somewhat of a respite. Engineer Otto Oertzen from HWK was responsible for installation of the Walter engines in the Me 163 A at Peenemünde West, and later in the Me 163B at Jesau, as well as for Ek16.

The remaining eight prototypes (the V6 through the V13) were built over the course of 1942. Some were transported to Peenemünde, where they aided the test team in their long road to the Me 163B. In July 1942 the V6 was delivered to Peenemünde with the rocket engine already installed, whereas the V7 was again lacking the engine due to shortages, as was the case with the V8, V9, and V10 in November of that year. In the meantime, the V5 had been destroyed in a crash landing on 25 August 1942. And on 16 October 1942 Heini Dittmar severely injured his spinal column when he landed the V12 in Augsburg, an injury which resulted in a two-year pause for the gifted test pilot. The injury was caused when, on final approach, a sudden wind shear slammed the plane hard down onto the ground. Dittmar was seriously hurt on impact (he shattered his fifth thoracic vertebra), since up until then the Me 163 was only equipped with a simple uncushioned seat. This was immediately corrected, with all aircraft being fitted with cushioned seats. From that point onward Rudolf Opitz assumed the role of chief test pilot. Shortly prior to this, on 5 October 1942, *Erprobungskommando 16* was established at Karlshagen.

The V11 and V12 arrived at Peenemünde in February 1943 by train, also minus their engines. Also in February, two engine systems were finally made available for the V7 and V8 and were installed. As 1943 continued Walter engines eventually arrived for the V9 through V11 test prototypes, with some of these being an improved version of the RII-203. The V11 completed its first flight with an installed rocket motor on 25 October 1943. The V12 and V13 prototypes were never kitted out with an engine.

Also in February 1943, the V8 served as a testbed for an exhaust rudder located in the exhaust path of the rocket engine in an effort to improve yaw control on takeoff and at low speeds; the Me 163 A's aerodynamic rudder was effectively worthless at these slower speeds. Furthermore, the summer of 1943 also saw a series of trials using attached solid-fuel booster rockets used for takeoff, each with a thrust of 250 kp.

At the end of the Me 163 A testing the six surviving aircraft were turned back over to EK 16 for training its pilots, and from there to *III Gruppe* of *Jagdgeschwader 400* in October 1944, when that unit was established in Upper Silesia.

Me 163B

The tests during the summer of 1941 and the record-setting flight on 2 October of that year increasingly stirred the interests of the RLM in the Me 163. Additionally, Hellmuth Walter had announced the development of an even more powerful rocket engine, the RII-211 (109-509) which, unlike the RII-203, would be a hot burning system. Therefore, Lippisch was to develop an operational design from the Me 163 A that would be suited as a rapid-climbing point defense interceptor. It was acknowledged that, given this role, a short operational period was acceptable. Thanks to the support of Ernst Udet, in the fall of 1941 a contract was issued for the construction of 70 pre-production Me 163B aircraft. Delivery was to take place by the summer of 1942, thus enabling the establishment of an operational fighter group by no later than the spring of 1943. Messerschmitt, however, had reservations regarding the operational readiness of the type by then, and ultimately was able to agree that the aircraft would be classified as prototypes. This offered the advantage of enabling changes and modifications at any time during its production.

Because of the numerous preparations undertaken by Lippisch and his colleagues, construction of the Me 163B actually began as early as October 1941. The wooden wings, with their sweepback of 23.5 degrees, remained unchanged from those of the Me 163 A, even though the RLM called for a metal wing as long as there was no shortage of materials. The fuselage was to be built of metal, with Messerschmitt's typical preference for monocoque construction coming into play here. Compared to the Me 163 A the fuselage would have to be enlarged in order to accept the more powerful engine, with its thrust of no less than 1,500 kp, a larger fuel tank system, military equipment, and armament (2 x MG 151/20 in the wing roots). The Me 163B's projected takeoff weight was around 3,300 kg. This took into account a fuel tank sized according to the HWK's calculated fuel consumption rate of 3 kg/s. There were effectively two options with regard to fuel burn: either a maximum throttle setting for the engine for 12 minutes or a 3 minute climb to 12,000 meters with a subsequent 30 minutes' flying time at reduced throttle and a speed of 950 km/h, giving a combat radius of 255 km.

Mainly due to Udet's strong support of the program, work on the Me 163B continued apace up until his suicide on 17 November 1941. The situation changed dramatically under Udet's successor, *Generalfeldmarschall* Milch. Almost immediately he reestablished the priorities within the aircraft armaments programs, to the disadvantage of the Me 163B, for this was unsuited for the Eastern Front, and Allied bombing raids were relatively rare at this date. Nevertheless, the Me 163B rolled out on schedule at the Augsburger *Versuchsbau* in April 1942. This was then given its check flight by Heini Dittmar on 26 June 1942 at Augsburg, albeit as an engine-less glider after being towed to altitude by an Me 110. The remaining 69 pre-production airplanes were completed at the Messerschmitt Works in Obertraubling (near Regensburg) and gradually delivered through the end of 1943. In mid-July the Me 163B V2 arrived at Peenemünde, again without an engine.

This program, too, encountered difficulties with rocket engines, and not just from the technological side, either. It was much more due to the supply (or more correctly, the lack thereof). Both the HWK RII-211 (109-509) from Hellmuth Walter in Kiel, as well as the P-3390A from BMW could never be delivered as scheduled, despite the fact that each company had its own prototype for studying installation options. This meant that the majority of the flight testing not directly associated with the powerplant was conducted by gliders. This included, for example, undercarriage (skid) testing, weapons testing, radio testing, braking parachute testing, and several other tests. The Me 163B continued to profit from the good handling qualities of the Me 163 A, despite the fact that spin trials revealed a problem with stability ("uncontrolled spinning"). An initial fix to the problem was to fit an adjustable leading edge slat to the wings, covering 40% of the span beginning from the tip. When this proved to be inadequate, the slat was replaced by a fixed gap (*C-Spalt*) along the forward edge of the outer wing. The result of this was that the aircraft could no longer even be put into a spin, even later when the engines were installed. Company testing of the type in its glider mode was carried out at Lechfeld. Subsequent engine and operational trials, on the other hand, were conducted at Peenemünde West and Karlshagen.

The changes discovered necessary during the course of the test program (e.g. adjusting the springs/shocks for the takeoff trolley, pilot's seat, and landing skid) were all gradually retroactively applied to every prototype by the Klemm Company in Böblingen. Here, too, the installation of the rocket motors was carried out in the pre-production aircraft. For this reason Klemm later assumed full-scale production of the B-series and the type's delivery to the *Luftwaffe*. After Heini Dittmar's serious accident in an Me 163 A at Augsburg in October 1942 the test team centered around Rudolf Opitz at Peenemünde, where he was joined by two industry pilots, Hans Boye and Bernhard Hohmann.

There were still no engines available by early 1943, and it was decided to take an HWK RII-203 from the Me 163 A program and install it in the Me 163B-0 V8. This allowed Rudolf Opitz to finally take to the air in an Me 163B-0 for the first rocket-powered flight on 21 February 1943.

Me 163B Design Description

Role:	single jet rocket powered point defense
Crew:	one pilot
Wings:	cantilever mid-wing wooden construction with 8 mm plywood skinning, self-supporting between ribs 2 and 7 to accommodate wing tanks. Two section, two spar wings of tapered design, attached to fuselage using three bolts each side. Leading edge sweep of 23.5 degrees, geometric offset of 5.7 degrees, angle of attack off the fuselage axis 3.33 degrees. Built in groove in wing leading edge 2.18 meters long, beginning about 30 cm from wing tip. Hydraulically activated landing flaps on wing underside made of wood with supplemental aluminum skinning. Fabric covered trim flaps on the inner wing trailing edge (between ribs 4 and 10).
Fuselage:	all-metal monocoque design of alloy metal, consisting of five components (armored nose section, forward section, upper cover, aft section, tail). The aft section is removable via quick release connectors to facilitate access to engine; oval fuselage cross section; aerodynamically blended using plates at all wing/fuselage join areas; armored cockpit (15 mm nose armor, 90 mm armored glass, 15 mm head and shoulder armor, 8 mm back armor), no pressurized cockpit, just a simple ram air intake. Entry via starboard opening jettisonable canopy. Vent hatch (poor weather viewport) incorporated into port side of canopy; special pilot suit to include overshoes, helmet and parachute pack
Control Surfaces:	fabric-covered combined elevator-ailerons (elevons) on the outer wing trailing edge (between ribs 11 and 18) with built-in trim tabs, central vertical stabilizer of wooden construction, fabric covered rudder with integral trim tab
Undercarriage:	jettisonable wheel assembly (1.50 m wheelbase; 700 x 175 tires; weight 80 kg), central shock- absorbed landing skid made of duraluminum framing with skid surface of steel plating; extendable/retractable via pneumatic hydraulic system; retractable tailwheel (260 x 85 tire)
Engine:	HWK 109-509 A-1 with five stage throttle (off, neutral, 1, 2, 3), thrust 100-1600 kp (for the Me 163B-1 variant the HWK 109-509 B with a thrust of 100-2000 kp was installed) Three *T-Stoff* tanks in fuselage and four *C-Stoff* tanks in the wings with a total capacity of 1,660 liters.
Military Equipment:	2 x MK 108 with 60 rounds of ammunition each, in wing roots, fired via button on KG12E knurled joystick, sighted to 500 meters Revi 16b standard gunsight FuG 16E transmitter/receiver with FuG 16ZE installation kit FuG 25a Identification Friend or Foe

Me 163B Tank System

Fuel	Location	Capacity (liters)
T-Stoff	tank area	1,040
	cockpit l/h	60
	cockpit r/h	60
C-Stoff	wing l/h	177
	wing r/h	177
	wing leading edge l/h	73
	wing leading edge r/h	73
	total fuel capacity	= 1,660
		(= 2,026 kg)

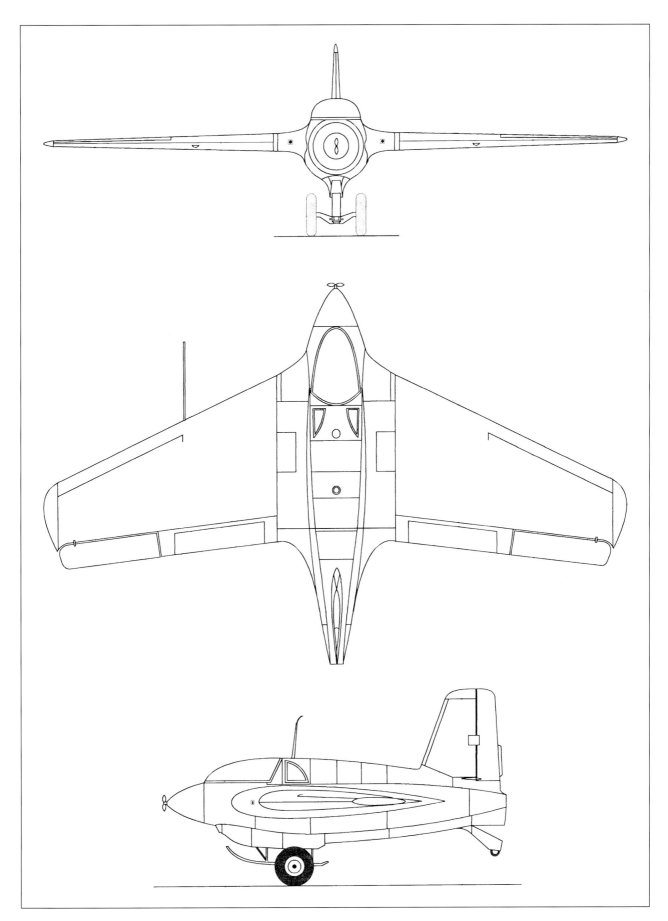

Messerschmitt Me 163 B

Me 163 B after its restoration by MBB. It now resides in the *Deutsches Museum* in Munich.

Me 163 B seen taking off.

Parallel to this, in early 1943 a BMW P 3390A rocket engine arrived, was duly installed in the Me 163B V10, and flown. Unlike the Walter engine, the BMW engine was based on nitric acid (*Sv-Stoff*) as the oxidizer and methanol (*M-Stoff*) for the propellant. However, there were problems with the fuel supply system, and the trials had to be abandoned in the end.

On 28 April 1943 the Department L at Messerschmitt AG was dissolved, and on 1 May 1943 Alexander Lippisch, due to repeated differences of opinion with Professor Messerschmitt, took five of his colleagues to work at the *Luftfahrtforschungsanstalt Wien* (Vienna Aviation Research Institute). The remaining 80 employees in Department L were distributed among the other departments based on their qualifications. Work on the Me 163 project continued without interruption under the direction of Rudolf Reutel. Nevertheless, the company was forced to tailor back the program somewhat in light of its other efforts. Alexander Lippisch continued his association with the Me 163 program in an advisory capacity.

The first HWK RII-211 engine was not available until June 1943, and was immediately put into the Me 163B-0 V21. By this time Messerschmitt had completed the entire B-0 pre-production batch at Obertraubling and had begun on the B-1 series. Following a number of ground runs, on 24 June 1943 Rudolf Opitz took to the air for the first time in the Me 163B0 V21. On takeoff, however, the uneven surface of the runway tore off the takeoff trolley and damaged the *T-Stoff* lines. Since breaking off the takeoff was out of the question at this point, Opitz continued the run on the plane's skid. After "sliding along" 100 meters he eventually broke free of the ground, but then the cockpit began filling up with *T-Stoff* steam as he climbed upward; all the instruments and the cockpit

Me 163 B-V2 minus a rocket engine.

49

Me 163 B-V8

Me 163 B on a transport trailer with its wings removed.

canopy became milky white. The moment of relief came after a flight time of 2 minutes, when the fuel ran out and the engine switched off. Immediately the steam ceased in the cockpit, and Opitz was able to end the flight without anything untoward occurring.

The Me 163's potential against Allied bomber formations was recognized in the summer of 1943, prompting Armaments Minister Albert Speer to raise the urgency of this program to "high." But as so often happens, the issue was immediately pushed to unrealistic proportions when the call went out for a constant supply of 1,000 Me 163B *Komets* (as the plane was known from that point on) as point defense fighters.

On 26 July 1943 an RAF Mosquito reconnaissance plane overflew Peenemünde and took several aerial photographs of the site. When the pictures were evaluated, tiny aircraft were discovered that were initially designated *Peenemünde 20*. This was the first time that the Allies (unwittingly) learned of the existence of the Me 163 A.

The Messerschmitt Works at Obertraubling were heavily bombed on 12 August 1943. This resulted in a cessation of Me 163B production in favor of the Me 109 assembly line. The entire program passed to the Klemm Company in Böblingen which, for its part, contracted with a number of decentralized subcontractors. The assembled Me 163Bs were brought by rail, first to Lechfeld and later to Jesau, for their check flights.

The Klemm company began delivering additional prototype planes converted to take the HWK RII-211 beginning in August 1943. But as the engine test phase of the program soon revealed, fuel consumption was too high. Initial test bench trials showed a consumption rate of 5 kg/s, compared with the calculated 3 kg/s. This meant that a fully tanked plane (1,550 kg *T-Stoff* and 470 kg *C-Stoff*) had an endurance of just 6 minutes at full thrust. In addition, the takeoff weight had risen to 4,300 kg, giving a wing loading of 220 kg/m^2. Furthermore, the engine test phase brought to light a series of technical problems, many of which

Me 163 B (*Bundesarchiv*)

were never resolved prior to the end of the war.. Among these was the engine's habit of independently shutting itself off when decelerating. It took two minutes before the engine could be restarted in the air, and there was no guarantee of an aerial restart being successful, forcing the pilot to land with a large quantity of fuel on board as a result. The takeoff trolley and landing skid also demanded additional time in flight operations. The trolley had to be attached before takeoff and recovered after being jettisoned. After landing, the aircraft rested helplessly on the ground until it could be transported off. The takeoff trolley was then reattached, until the *Scheuschlepper* became available. This was a tractor designed in-house and named for its inventor.

Not to be forgotten was the handling of the extremely dangerous *T-* and *C-Stoff* fuels, which could only be stored in special containers. *T-Stoff* would react with a violent explosion at the slightest disturbance, and even the smallest amount of the spilled liquid had to be washed away with large amounts of water, which is the reason why, after engine shutoff, the remaining quantities of the fuel (70 to 150 liters) posed a latent risk of explosion during each and every landing. To simplify handling and to improve safety, all *T-Stoff* containers were marked in white and all *C- Stoff* containers in yellow. Additionally, the fuel trucks were indicated by a large "T" and "C," respectively, and could only ever be within 800 meters of each other at any given time. The same markings were also applied to all fuel tanks and fuel connectors on the airplane.

Prior to every refuelling, the entire engine was thoroughly rinsed off inside and out with water in order to flush out any remaining fuel. Furthermore, during refueling the whole airplane was sprayed with water to immediately neutralize any spilled or dripping fuel.

To protect the pilot and ground personnel from the highly aggressive *T-Stoff*, a gray-green flight suit was developed out of non-organic asbestos/synthetic rubber or polycarbonate fabric. The *T-Stoff*, however, could leak through the seams if given enough time.

Startup of the rocket engine was, according to a description by Mano Ziegler, accomplished as follows:

"The engine itself consisted of a feed system, the governor, and the combustion chamber. To start it, a switch activated an electric motor, which in turn drove a small turbine and fed a small amount of T-Stoff into the steam generator. When the electric motor was turned off the turbine was driven by the generator and then pumped T- and C-Stoff from the tanks into the governor system. This was in a ratio of 1 to 3. A pressure balance controlled the ratio, and the fuel was fed through 12 lines into the combustion chamber at the end of the fuselage, where it entered via nozzles fitted with back pressure valves. When the liquids—now atomized—combined, there occurred a steady explosion-like combustion in a jet of flame, whose pressure was about 24 kg/cm² of atmospheric excess pressure. Combustion was controlled via the governor system—the throttle—in the cockpit; when the lever was pushed forward the generator initially fed more T-Stoff, and the throttle was opened so wide that C-Stoff, too, could flow in. This C-Stoff, preheated as it passed over the combustion chamber's cooling mantle, then regulated the quantity of T-Stoff in the pressure scale. At full throttle the entire supply of fuel—about two metric tons—was consumed in four to five minutes. At sea level, performance of the engine was around 4,500 hp, with this more than doubling at altitudes of 10,000 to 14,000 meters. And for all this the whole engine didn't weigh more than 150 kg.

New engines were tested for their functionality using water. This meant that the C- and T-Stoff tanks were filled with water, which was pushed through the tubes by the steam generator. If all the tubes were sealed and the water pressed out of the tanks in 4 or 5 minutes, then the engine was considered to be in order according to human calculations.

T- and C-Stoff were water soluble, and since T-Stoff in particular would set on fire any organic thing it came in contact with, there was always a fireman on hand with a water hose standing next to the airplane to immediately neutralize any T-Stoff running out."

The entire startup operation for the Me 163B was done according to the following steps:

1. Turn on electrical system
2. Check the play of the rudders and flaps
3. Set elevators tailheavy by 3-6 degrees
4. Put on oxygen mask and check
5. Close and lock canopy
6. Start engine using battery starter
7. Move gas lever from 'off' to "neutral," and activate starter knob until turbine is running (takes 4-5 seconds), which sets the turbine pumps in motion. This in turn releases a small amount of *T-* and *C-Stoff* into the combustion chamber, which converts this into high pressure steam and then is used to drive the fuel pumps via the steam turbine.
8. The engine starts automatically at a turbine r.p.m. of between 40 and 50 percent
9. Check instruments and set throttle control to stage 1, then to stage 2
10. Check instruments and set throttle control to stage 3 (full)
11. Aircraft rolls over its small chocks and picks up speed
12. Acceleration continues and plane lifts off at 280 km/h
13. Release takeoff trolley at an altitude of 8 to 10 meters by retracting the extended skid
14. Accelerate to 800 km/h (speed at end of runway) and then climb almost vertically at 700 km/h

The climb out takes place at a speed of 700 km/h, which equates to a time-to-climb to 12,000 meters' altitude of about three minutes, a rate of approximately 70 m/s—an incredible value in an age when propeller-driven fighter planes "sluggishly" bored their way upward (the climb rate for the Me 109G was about 17 m/s).

Experiments with a rocket-powered trolley and supplemental solid fuel booster rockets were carried out in an effort to increase the limited range of the type, but these were soon abandoned.

The normal service ceiling of the Me 163B was set at 12,000 meters, since the type did not have a pressurized cockpit, but in spite of this the pilots underwent special high altitude training on the Zugspitze and in a captured Russian high altitude chamber (so that they could recognize the specific symptoms of altitude sickness). In addition, the pilots were fed a special diet. During one test the Me 163B V14 climbed to an altitude of 15,000 meters on 12 October 1944, with the pilot making use of a captured American oxygen system.

The maximum level speed of the Me 163B was 965 km/h. The Me 163B never achieved the magical 1,000 km/h limit, because compressibility problems would always set in beforehand, causing the aircraft to begin shuddering. The airplane would then start to roll from side to side until the nose suddenly dropped down, an act linked to the engine shutting down of its own volition. It was impossible for the pilot to bail out at a speed above 400 km/h, because the airflow prevented the canopy from opening. Landing approach—unpowered—took place at a speed of 225 km/h, reducing to 160 km/h by the time of touchdown.

Several important changes were introduced beginning with the 51st aircraft of the B-0 series, including a vent on the left side of the cockpit canopy (particularly useful for removing steam) and a fuel dump for the fuel system that could release the entire quantity of *T-Stoff* in 1.5 minutes.

In late 1943 the *Versuchsbau Me 163* was removed from the Augsburg-Haunstetten and Obertraubling Works and relocated to the airfield at Laupheim. After this site was heavily bombed on 19 July 1944 the *Versuchsbau*, under the management of Johann B. Kaiser, diverted to the fortress at Kronach, but it never resumed its work.

In June 1944 it finally became possible to prove the structural reliability of the aircraft in flight. The requirement was for a pullout maneuver with a load of 6 *g* at a speed of 700 km/h and 880 km/h. Test pilot *Olt* Heinz Peters in Me 163B-V41 in fact demonstrated a load of 7.1 *g* at a speed of 650 km/h and 7.5 *g* at 890 km/h. *Olt* Peters was a glider pilot instructor on the

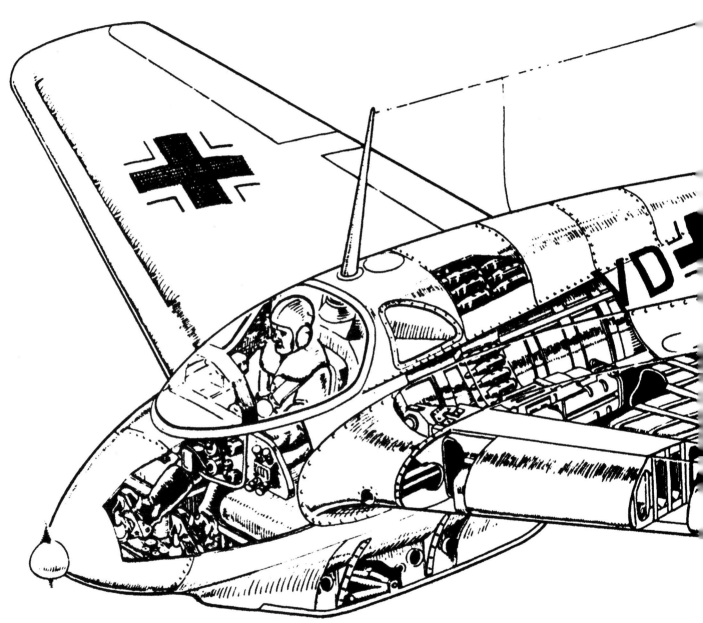

Me 163 cutaway

Wasserkuppe before the war and had beefed up the Opitz/Dittmar—who had sought him out—from early 1944 onward.

In February 1945 the OKL stopped full-scale production of the Me 163B. A total of 364 Me 163Bs were manufactured, 279 in series production, with 42 of these being built in 1945. But only a quarter of these would eventually become operational. There are still 10 Me 163s in museums around the world today. One of these is in the *Deutsches Museum* in Munich, and another in the *Luftwaffenmuseum* in Berlin.

After the war, Major Späte offered the following assessment of the Me 163:

"...vastly superior to enemy aircraft in terms of performance; faster, cheaper to produce, better climb, unconstrained by altitude and a new fighter type, the interceptor (which intercepted the enemy). From a flight handling standpoint, the Me 163 was the most beautiful you could imagine. From 150 to 1,000 km/h the control surfaces were so well balanced in their forces and effect that you'd be hard pressed to find another plane like it. Despite its unique tailless planform, the Me 163 was stable in every axis. This meant that at high speeds you could effortlessly make any course correction, in any direction, something that is of major significance for a fighter plane and is quite often lacking in other faster airplanes. Behind these qualities was the brilliant design work of Dr. Lippisch, as well as many years of self-denying systematic de-velopmental work, and last but not least the exemplary flying of the machine by Heini Dittmar."

Erprobungskommando 16 (EK 16) and JG 400

In April 1942 *Hauptmann* Wolfgang Späte (who was a famous glider pilot before the war) of II/JG 54 was named as the type overseer for the Me 163 and, on the orders of *General der Jagdflieger* Galland dated 20 April 1942 was assigned the responsibility of setting up EK 16 at Peenemünde to ensure that the military's interests were met before it was introduced into front line service. After being briefed by Heini Dittmar, Späte made his first flight in an Me 163 A on 11 May 1942.

After just a few weeks EK 16 counted among its ranks several experienced fighter pilots, including:

Olt Joschi Pöhs (JG 54)
Olt Johan Kiel (ZG 26)
Olt Rudolf Opitz
Olt Herbert Langer
Hptm Toni Thaler

Flying was done with those Me 163 As already on hand, as well as the ones that were gradually arriving.

In the summer of 1942 Hanna Reitsch also came to EK 16, where in addition to her Berlin desk work was to assume the flight check program for those Me 163 B-0 production aircraft built at the Messerschmitt Works in Obertraubling. But her first flight with the

| | | | Prototypes |
Type No.	Factory No.	Code	Comments
Me 163B V1	163 100 10	VD+EK	Used to test the longer tailskid that was ultimately used on production versions
Me 163B V2	163 100 11	VD+EL	
Me 163B V3		VD+EM	
Me 163B V4			
Me 163B V5			
Me 163B V6		CE+RE	HWK 109-509 A-2 testing for the Me 163C
Me 163B V7			
Me 163B V8			
Me 163B V9			
Me 163B V10			Used to test the BMW P3390A and the "Latscher undercarriage" with improved shock absorption
Me 163B V16			Testing of RATO boosters under the supervision of Heini Dittmar
Me 163B V18			Testing of the HWK 109-509 A-2 for the Me 163C, later converted to the Me 163D at Junkers
Me 163B V21		VA+SS	First to be fitted with an HWK RII-211 engine
Me 163B V41		PK+QL	Structural stress testing in June of 1944
Me 163B V45			Testing of the *Jägerfaust*
Me 163B V61		GN+ND	

Me 163 B-0 (towed behind an Me 110) ended in a crash landing. After takeoff the trolley would not come free because it had jammed. This meant that Hanna Reitsch had to land on its wheels. But her approach was too steep, and she touched down in a field ahead of the runway. There, however, the ground was so soft that the trolley sank into it more than normal; the resulting braking effect caused the airplane to flip over. Reitsch suffered a broken skull and other injuries, for she had not been wearing a seat belt. For the experienced aviatrix, this meant a break in flying for several months.

In addition to tracking development, a core task of EK 16 was the initial training of about 30 pilots and the requisite technical maintenance personnel. Personnel were broken down into the following groups:

Management:
Hptm Wolfgang Späte
Pilots:
Olt Franz Medicus
Lt Hans Bott
Lt Franz Rösle
Lt Fritz Kelb
Lt Mano Ziegler
Fw Rolf "Bubi" Glogar, etc.
Instructor:
Rudolf Opitz

Doctors:
OSA Dr. Helmut Dyckerhoff
Dr. Erich Dunker
Engine:
Olt Otto Oertzen
Weapons Testing:
Olt August Hachtel
(Experience with the Ju 87 against Russian tanks)

Once unpowered trials at Lagerlechfeld had concluded around the end of 1942, these first engine-less Me 163Bs were made available to EK 16.

Peenemünde was heavily bombed during the night of 17/18 August 1943, with most of the damage concentrated in the eastern section; Peenemünde West was left virtually untouched. EK 16 was subsequently moved to Anklam, on the mainland directly across from the island of Usedom, and a short time later to Bad Zwischenahn, near Oldenburg, where training operations resumed. Pilot training on the Me 163B adhered to the following pattern:

1. Glider flying school at Gelnhausen (*Kranich*, *Grunau Baby*, *Rhönsperber*, *Habicht* with 13.60 m wingspan, *Habicht* with 8.0 m wingspan, and finally the *Stummelhabicht* with 6.0 m wingspan, whose landing speed was 100 km/h)

Cutaway of the Me 163 showing the weapons configuration to good effect.

57

2. Me 163 A (towed flight, gliding empty, gliding with limited ballast, gliding with full weight, rocket-powered takeoff)
3. Me 163B (gliding empty, gliding with full weight, rocket-powered takeoff)

The most important goal in glider training was the successful execution of precision landings despite the high approach speeds.

The first two-seat Me 163S trainer (non-powered) was not made available until December 1944.

By September 1943 EK 16 had grown to about 150 personnel (including five flying instructors and 23 students).

On 30 December 1943 the Me 163 A-V8 was involved in a serious accident that once again highlighted the danger of the chemicals used as fuels. Joschi Pöhs dropped the trolley too soon after takeoff. It bounced back up and damaged the *T-Stoff* lines, which caused the engine to immediately shut down. Pöhs pulled the plane around to make an immediate landing, but he was too low and clipped a *Flak* tower with his wingtip. The plane crashed from an altitude of 30 meters, sliding along another 50 meters until it came to rest. There was no explosion, nor did a fire break out. It didn't appear to be too disastrous, especially since the fire crew arrived at the site of the crashed plane within a minute. But when they went to pull the pilot out, he was no longer there. The *T-Stoff* running out of the broken lines had made its way into the cockpit and had dissolved the (hopefully unconscious) Joschi Pöhs.

In early January 1944 EK 16 at last received the first three of a total of 12 completely equipped Me 163B operational machines, although these had not yet been checked out. This was nearly two years after delivery of the first type, the Me 163B-0 V1. Gradually the remaining pre-production aircraft arrived at EK 16, where they were initially put to use in the training role. The first 40 aircraft carried V designations and were painted light gray. Armament of the first 45 planes was the MG 151/20. This switched from the 46th aircraft onward to the MK 108. Beginning with aircraft no. 71 the planes were built by the Klemm Company and were accordingly designated the Me163B-1a.

Except for the first 12 pre-production airplanes, all machines arrived at EK 16 and the later operational units with their factory check flights completed. To accomplish this, an internal "check flight detachment" was established in September 1943 at Jesau, a peacetime airfield of the *Luftwaffe* 22 km southeast of Königsberg, in East Prussia. The planes were delivered there by train, and the group consisted of three civilian pilots (Karl Voy, Franz Perschall, and *Herr* Lamm). Technical acceptance of the aircraft consisted of two to three towed flights behind an Me 110, followed by glider flights, and one to two live rocket-powered takeoffs. The airplanes were then sent to EK 16, where they were test flown before being distributed to the various operational units. After an accident involving the pilot Lamm, and because of the increasing deliveries of production aircraft, the check flight detachment was reinforced by *Lt* Ziegler and *Fw* Nelte. Technical supervision of the acceptance flight program fell to *Ing.* Otto Oertzen.

In late January 1944 the OKL ordered the establishment of an Me 163 operational unit to be created from components of EK 16. Initially, this was set up as *20 Staffel* of *Jagdgeschwader 1* (20./JG 1) at Bad Zwischenahn, with a planned inventory of 12 Me 163Bs. Squadron commander was Robert Olejnik. By February 1944, though, the unit was redesignated 1./JG 400 and transferred to Wittmundhafen on 1 March. At that time the squadron consisted of 12 pilots. The first aircraft did not arrive until March 1944.

Since there will be several appearances of unit designations of the German *Luftwaffe* over the coming pages, at this point a brief discussion of a *Luftwaffe* unit's composition is in order.

A *Jagdgeschwader*, or wing, within the *Luftwaffe* had precisely 90 aircraft, which were distributed among three *Gruppen*, or groups, of 27 aircraft each, and a *Stab*, or staff. Each *Gruppe*, for its part, comprised of three *Staffeln* (squadrons) of nine airplanes each. On hand were also up to 30 replacement aircraft.

The smallest flying units within the *Staffel* were the *Rotte* and the *Kette*, consisting of two and three aircraft each, respectively.

In April 1944 2./JG 400 was established—on paper at least—at Oranienburg, with *Hauptmann* Böhner serving as squadron commander. This unit later moved to Venlo.

According to EK 16, by May 1944 the ME 163B-0 pre-production versions had reached operational readiness, and work could now begin on combat methodology. The Me 163's flight performance was fundamentally different than that of propeller driven fighters, and the combat methods used for the latter type simply could not translate to the rocket fighter. EK 16 developed the following profile for the Me 163B against Allied bombers:

1. Takeoff
2. Climb to 11,000 m at 700 km/h in 5:45 mins, throttling the engine back to neutral about 1,500 meters before reaching operational altitude to avoid negative acceleration effect on engine.
3. Continue level flight
4. Once enemy is acquired, accelerate to 900 km/h
5. Attack from behind and 1,000 m above at a speed of at least 930 km/h to avoid becoming a victim of the escort fighters (for example, the P-51 Mustang and P-47 Thunderbolt)
6. Break off attack no later than 200 m from the target and roll away
7. After passing the enemy, regain altitude for the second attack

Since the Me 163B could reach enemy aircraft just two or three minutes after taking off, takeoff did not occur until the enemy was in visible range. This ensured that, after reaching the enemy, the airplane would have a flight time under rocket power of about four minutes.

Naturally, this method in no way resembled the standard fighter attack profiles then current in the *Luftwaffe*, which had been tailored to the much slower Me 109 and Fw 190 piston-engined fighters. For this reason the Me 163B aircraft were separately directed by *Würzburg* systems when operating. Various direction methods, such as the "*Egon*" method and the "*Y*" method, were tried out, with *Olt* Gustaf Korff of EK 16 playing a major role in their development. The Achilles' heel of such operations was, however, the landing approach. The unpowered final approach began at an altitude of about 1,500 meters, where the speed was just 300 km/h. This meant that an airplane in this phase was easy prey for Allied fighters. Unlike Me 262 units, which faced similar problems (though) in the takeoff stage, Me 163 units seldom enjoyed friendly fighter protection provided by Me 109s and Fw 190s over their home airfield.

On 13 May 1944 the first official combat operation of the Me 163 took place against American bombers with escort (Republic P-47 Thunderbolts, in this case). On this occasion, *Major* Späte had his Me 163B-0 V41 painted red, with a nod to the Fokker *Dreidecker* of Baron Manfred von Richthofen. He sighted two American Thunderbolts. But on his initial pass the engine died, a victim of negative acceleration, just at the moment Späte attempted to pass the two planes to gain a better position. Fortunately for him, the two had not spotted him yet. After the requisite two-minute wait he started the engine again, but on the second run the machine passed 810 km/h and suddenly dropped over onto its left wing as transonic shock waves began building up.

It was at this critical point, in late May 1944, that *Major* Späte (who had become *Kommodore* of JG 400 in the interim) was again transferred back to JG 54 and replaced by *Oberst* Gordon Gollob who, although an excellent fighter pilot, had no experience whatsoever with rocket-powered aircraft.

Bad Zwischenahn was bombed on 30 May 1944, causing EK 16 to divert to Brieg, on the Oder, for a few days until the runway could be repaired.

Oberst Gollob saw the advantages of the Me 163 primarily as a point defense fighter. Unlike *Major* Späte, who wanted to spread the *Staffel* out to build a wide defensive belt against the Allied bomber streams. This involved individual bases distributed at intervals of about 100 km in order to simultaneously cover all Allied bomber routes. For this reason, infrastructures were already being built at Venlo, Deelen, Bad Zwischenahn, Wittmundhafen, Nordholz, and Husum. But Gollob moved both *Staffeln* of JG 400 to Brandis, near Leipzig, where KG 1 had been based earlier. There, though, no preparations whatsoever had been made for the Me 163's arrival, so that fuel, for example, had to be stored above ground in railroad tankers. There 1./JG 400 was formed, with Olejnik as commander, by combining 1./JG 400 and 2./JG 400. Its mission was to protect the Leuna Works about 50 km away, which produced synthetic fuels and rubber products. This would involve massed takeoffs, with the rocket fighters departing in 20 second intervals, which of necessity would also result in massed landings with immobile aircraft on the field.

On 28 July 1944 I./JG 400 carried out its first mission, against 569 B-17 bombers of the U.S. 8th Air Force attacking the Leuna Works. This mission brought to light yet another problem with using the high speed rocket fighter. Because of the great speed advantage enjoyed by the Me 163—around 500 km/h faster than the bombers—and the MK 108's maximum range of 600 m, pilots only had about 3 to 4 seconds of effective engagement time. Given the MK 108's rate of fire at 660 rounds per minute, this meant that only a few rounds could be fired before the attack had to be broken off at a minimum distance of 200 meters from the target.

This was one of the reasons behind the development of a new type of weapon, the so called "*Jägerfaust*" (fighter's fist) or, as it was officially known, the SG 500. This was in part based on the initiative of Dr. Langweiler, the inventor of the German *Panzerfaust*.

The SG 500 was a vertically fired weapon mounted in the wings. The firing tubes were loaded with missiles (50 mm caliber) having an explosive charge about the same as that of the German 88 mm anti-aircraft shell. The weapon fired automatically, triggered by a selenium cell when the aircraft passed beneath a target. With the approval of *General der Jagdflieger* Galland, the weapon was first successfully tested in the summer of 1944 at Werneuchen using an Fw 190, which had been fitted with one tube in each wing. The selenium cells were located on the wing leading edges. For testing the device, a large cloth measuring 50 meters x 2 meters was suspended between two tethered balloons, which Lt. Hachtel underflew at over 400 km/h in the Fw 190. The number of tubes per wing was gradually increased until there were four in each. Using these, Hachtel scored up to seven hits on the cloth per attack. The goal then became to fit up to five firing tubes into each wing of the Me 163B. The first to receive the weapon was Me 163B-0 V45. Into each wing was built five tubes clustered loosely together. To prevent all tubes from firing at the same time, delay timers were fitted into every second tube on each wing to avoid the air pressure from the muzzles becoming too strong. Flight testing initially took place without live ammunition to check out the flight handling and test the sensors. Tether balloons were again used until the RLM forbade them out of concern for

security. In their place were used two poles separated by about 30 meters, with a cloth (10 m x 2 m) stretched vertically between the two at a height of 20 meters. On Christmas Day 1944 *Lt.* Gustav Hachtel took off for the first time with the the V45 fully armed. He flew toward the poles at a speed of about 900 km/h, activating the selenium cells about 300 m before reaching them. But a low hanging cloud caused all the charges to fire simultaneously—somebody had forgotten to insert the delay timers in the tubes. This caused the canopy to blow off. *Lt.* Hachtel was just able to land the plane, but as he jumped out to save himself he broke his spinal column. *Lt.* Kelb successfully continued the test program using another Me 163B. By the end of the war, though, only 12 other machines were able to be fitted with the SG 500. The first and probably only live operation by an Me 163B so equipped took place by *Lt.* Kelb on 10 April 1945 against British Lancasters, reputedly bringing down one of their number.

In August 1944 the sole *C-Stoff* plant in Germany was completely destroyed in a bombing raid against HWK in Kiel and was not rebuilt by the end of the war, which subsequently caused severe restrictions in the Me 163B's operations, since only the inventory from widely dispersed depots were available for consumption, and only then until gone. The supply was transported via rail and, due to the increasing bombing raids on the rail system and the ever present danger of fighter-bombers, the fuel was often poorly produced, or so long in coming that it sometimes never arrived at its destination. Or if it did, it had dissolved and was therefore unusable.

In October 1944 JG 400's *Ergänzungsstaffel* (responsible for pilot training) in Udetfeld, East Prussia, had become so skilled that they were redesignated as III./JG 400, consisting of two *Staffel*, 13 *Staffel* under *Olt* Adolf Niemeyer and 14 *Staffel* under *Lt* Mano Ziegler. III./JG 400 was only equipped with the Me 163 A. One of the features 13./JG 400 successfully tested was arming the Me 163 with R4M rockets. These unguided 55 mm *Orkan* (Hurricane) R4M rockets had a length of 812 mm and contained 520 g of explosives. Maximum effective range of the rocket was 1,500 m, during which it attained a velocity of 525 km/s.

Olt Niemeyer "borrowed" a few R4M rockets from a rocket testing detachment located at the same airfield. Live testing began without much extra effort involved. Over a four week period there were several "live fire" evaluation flights carried out, with configurations of up to 24 R4M rockets being carried on a single Me 163 A. Results were most satisfactory, but by this time the new weapon could not be put into production in the numbers needed. In addition, this tiny rocket had the advantage of having a flight trajectory virtually identical to that of the MK 108 rounds, which meant that the Revi 16b gunsight required no adjustment and mixed armament could be carried.

In November 1944 *Major* Späte returned to the unit from Russia at the behest of *General* Galland, and once again assumed responsibilities as commander of JG 400.

On 12 December 1944 II./JG 400 under *Hptm.* Opitz was formed (on paper), consisting of *5 Staffel* under *Lt.* Franz Woidich and *6 Staffel* under *Lt.* Peter Gerth. The unit was located at Stargard for the protection of the hydro plants at Pölltz.

Because of the advancing Soviet troops, Udetfeld had to be evacuated in January 1945. III..JG 400 initially moved to Grottau, and then also to Brandis a short time afterward.

The aviation industry supplied the *Luftwaffe* with 90 Me 163 Bs in December 1944. The result of this was, that in January 1945, there were at least 100 Me 163 Bs parked in the surrounding forests, but fuel shortages precluded them from flying any more missions.

In January 1945 II./JG 400 was also forced to move from Stargard to Salzwedel to avoid the advancing Soviet forces. This base, however, was wholly unsuitable for Me 163 operations, and a short time later one squadron was disbursed to Bad Zwischenahn, another to Husum in Schleswig-Holstein (near the Danish border), and a third, along with the staff unit, to Nordholz, near Bremerhaven. At the end of March 1945 the rest of II./JG 400 also moved to Husum. On 22 April 1945 II./JG 400 flew against British Lancaster bombers en route to Bremen, their first mission. On 8 May 1945 II./JG 400 surrendered to British troops.

I./JG 400 was disbanded in late March 1945, with its personnel being distributed among various *Luftwaffe* divisions and used in the ground fighting against the advancing Soviet troops.

In all, the Me 163 accounted for a total of 12 confirmed kills while losing six at the hands of enemy aircraft.

The total tally of losses for the Me 163 B was as follows:

80%	on takeoff and landing
15%	due to onboard fire or loss of control at too high dive speeds
5%	due to enemy action

Me 163C

In early 1944 Hellmuth Walter began work on the 109-509 A-2 rocket engine that, in addition to the main combustion chamber with 1,700 kp thrust, also made use of a cruise combustion chamber having an output of 300 kp thrust. This dual-chambered engine stretched the burn time out to 9 minutes once the 10,000 m operating altitude had been reached. The first units were available in the spring of 1944 and were incorporated into two Me 163 B-0s (V6 and V18), which successfully tested the engines. The V6 was also equipped with a pressurized cockpit.

Because of the good test results, the RLM decided to proceed with the development of the Me 163C, which would be built around the new HWK 109-509 A-2 engine. To this end, the wings of the B-series would be utilized without modification. The fuselage, however, would require stretching to 7.04 meters, since the two MK 108s would now be incorporated into the fuselage, and the fuel tank capacity would be increased to accommodate the greater range. The goal for the C-version was a maximum operating time of 14 minutes at an altitude of 12,000 meters, on the assumption that the 12,000 m operating altitude could be reached in three minutes (climb angle of 40-45 degrees). Additional plans called for a pressurized cockpit, with the canopy being replaced by a design offering better all-round visibility to improve the pilot's view. Nevertheless, the landing skid would be retained, meaning that a major disadvantage of the B-series would carry over. All this led to a takeoff weight of 5,100 kg which, because of the increased fuel consumption this necessitated, ultimately resulted in a further reduction in range.

Three prototypes of the C-series were completed and tested by the *Oberbayerische Forschungsanstalt* in Oberammergau. But the C-series never went into production, since work on the project was overtaken by the D-series.

Me 163D

In the late summer of 1944 the Junkers Works were awarded a contract for developing a successor to the Me 163 B, which was designated the Ju 248.

One of the Me 163's most serious problems were the jettisoning wheels takeoff carried over from the DFS 194 and the landing on a sprung skid. The problem with this configuration was that the Me 163 had to take off directly into the wind, which meant that at low speeds the rudder was completely ineffective (since it was designed to operate at higher speeds). Furthermore, the narrow track undercarriage had a tendency to magnify every rough spot in the terrain. In order to carry out developmental research, in October 1944 Junkers planned to modify two Me 163s, the B-V13 and V18, by lengthening the fuselage and incorporating a steerable fixed tricycle undercarriage.

The necessary conversion of these aircraft to the so-called D-series was to have been completed by late 1944. Indeed, before the year was out the V18 underwent taxi testing, as well as several towed flights and landings.

The V13's conversion was not completed by the war's end, however. American troops found the aircraft on 19 April 1945 in Pölzen, where it was being prepared to accept the fuselage extension plug.

Me 163S

The high wing loading of the Me 163 B and the resulting high landing speeds naturally caused pilot trainees considerable problems.

Therefore, in early 1944 the RLM decided to create a two-seat non-powered training variant, the Me 163S, derived from the Me 163 B operational version. This meant removing the engine and the fuel cells from the fuselage. In their place went a second cockpit fitted with all instrumentation and control inputs.

Because of the absence of an engine, the Me 163S was lighter than the B-version and thus easier to land, since landing speeds were slower. By filling the wing tanks with water it was possible to gradually increase the landing weight to that of the Me 163 B, which meant that the higher landing approach and speed could be achieved at the same time.

Conversion of production versions from the B-series to the S-variant was done by Deutsche Lufthansa in Berlin Staaken. The first machine was completed in the summer of 1944, and in August of that year was towed in flight to JG 400 at Brandis with *Olt* Heinz Peters at the controls.

It was planned to convert 42 Me 163 Bs, but in all probability only about seven Me 163S trainer gliders were ever completed.

Soviet troops captured at least one flight-ready Me 163S that, after the war, was tested by the *Flugtechnisches Institut (LII)* and used for pilot training.

Me 263/Ju 248

The Me 163 B had two serious problems. On the one hand, its flight endurance was too short, and on the other it had a skid undercarriage, meaning that after landing the aircraft simply had to sit immobile on the field until the tow tractor came along. There were efforts with the C-version to increase the flight time, but the results were unsatisfactory.

Me 163C Design Description

Role:	single jet rocket powered point defense
Crew:	one pilot
Wings:	same as Me 163B
Fuselage:	all-metal monocoque design of alloy metal; The aft section is removable via quick release connectors to facilitate access to engine; oval fuselage cross section; aerodynamically blended using plates at all wing/fuselage join areas; armored cockpit, no pressurized cockpit, just a simple ram air intake. Entry via starboard opening jettisonable canopy.
Control Surfaces:	same as Me 163B
Undercarriage:	same as Me 163B
Engine:	HWK 109-509 A-2 with controllable thrust from 200-2000 kp (main engine 200-1,700 kp, cruise engine 300 kp)
	Several *T-Stoff* tanks in fuselage and *C-Stoff* tanks in the wings
Military Equipment:	2 x MK 108 blended into fuselage
	Revi 16b standard gunsight
	FuG 16E transmitter/receiver with FuG 16ZE installation kit
	FuG 25a Identification Friend or Foe

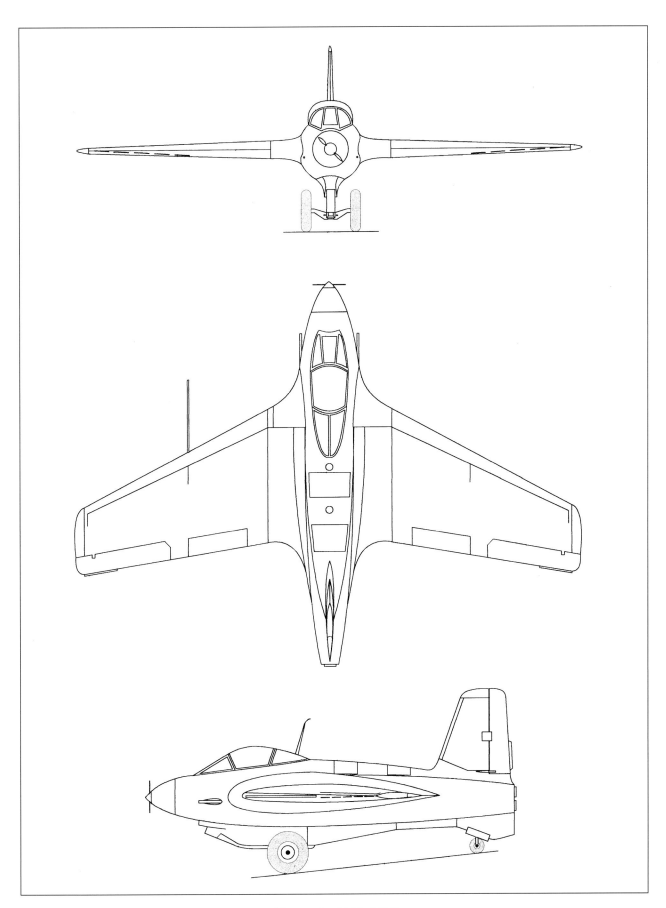

Messerschmitt Me 163 C

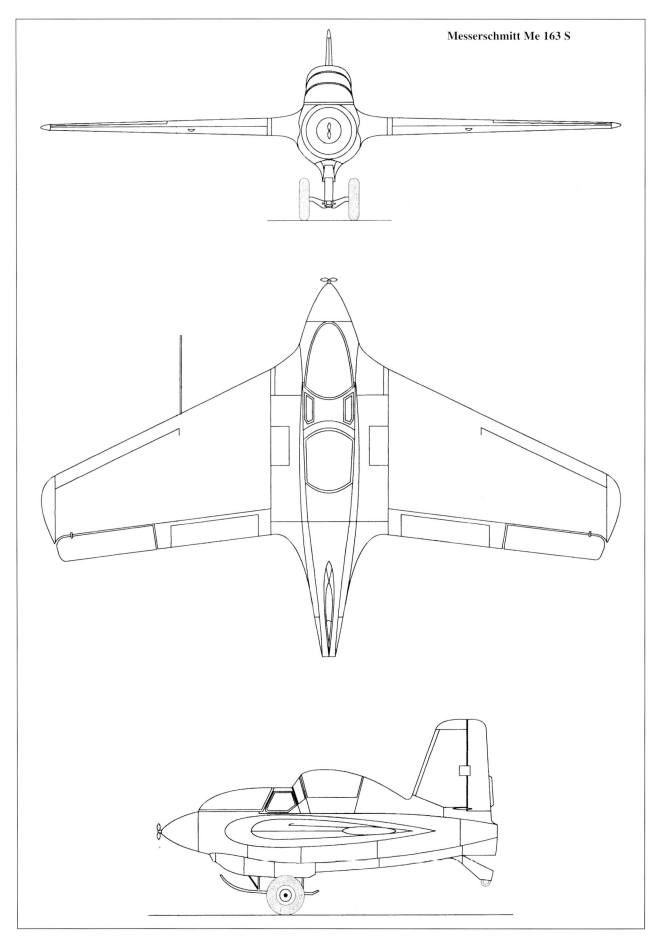

Messerschmitt Me 163 S

As a result, in the late summer of 1944 the RLM decided to have a successor model to the Me 163 developed. At this time, Messerschmitt was concentrating fully on the production of the Me 262, tying up its developmental resources to the fullest. Because of this, the contract went to the Junkers Werke, where the project was known as the Ju 248 under the direction of Prof. Hertel. Details for transferring responsibility for follow-on development, production, and oversight of the program were worked out directly between Messerschmitt and Prof. Hertel in August 1944. Official takeover of the program by the Junkers Works occurred on 1 September 1944.

Prof. Hertel, with the approval of the RLM, decided to skip the Me 163C then in development and build an entirely new airplane derived from the Me 163 B. The airplane would feature an all-metal fuselage with pressurized cockpit and a retractable tricycle landing gear. The pressurized cockpit was designed for an operating altitude of 8,000 to 15,000 meters above sea level. The necessary compressor was supplied by a generator driven by a small propeller in the nose. Furthermore, the new design would make use of the more powerful HWK 109-509C rocket engine with 400-2,400 kp of thrust (main chamber with 400-2,000 kp and cruise chamber with 400 kp), although this was never completed before the war's end. In addition, the fuel tank system would be expanded to a total of 2,440

liters (1,600 liters of *T-Stoff* and 840 liters of *C-Stoff*). This would theoretically give a flight time of 15 minutes at a speed of 700 km/h at 11,000 meters.

Other plans included beefing up the cockpit armor, with 20 mm thick plates in the leg area and alongside the fuselage, 12 mm for the upper body, and 20 mm for head and shoulders, pus a 100 mm thick bullet-proof glass.

The wings, rudder, and a large part of the equipment would be taken directly from the Me 163 B in order to save time in development. The raised side-opening canopy would come from the C-series, ensuring good all-round view for the pilot.

As already mentioned in detail in the section on the Me 163D, the Me 163 B V18 was converted to serve as the prototype for the Ju 248, and beginning in December 1944 pilot Heinz Peters tested it while being towed behind an Me 110. Even the V18, with all these conversions, demonstrated excellent handling qualities.

In October 1944 the design of the Ju 248 had been finalized. Upon instructions from the RLM, the aircraft was redesignated the Me 263 (RLM designation: 8-263) in order to highlight that this was a successor to the Me 163.

When the Me 163C program was halted the RLM issued a contract in late 1944 to Junkers for the construction of 20 Me 263 prototypes and 962 production

Messerschmitt Me 263-V1 at Junkers in Dessau. (photo: Radinger)

Me 263 Design Description

Role:	single jet rocket powered point defense
Crew:	one pilot
Wings:	cantilever mid-wing wooden construction with plywood skinning. Two section, two spar wings of tapered design, attached to fuselage using three bolts each side. Leading edge sweep of 23.5 degrees. Automatic leading edge slats. Hydraulically activated landing flaps on wing underside made of wood with supplemental aluminum skinning. Fabric covered trim flaps on the inner wing trailing edge.
Fuselage:	all-metal monocoque design of alloy metal, consisting of five components (armored nose section, forward section, upper cover, aft section, tail). The aft section is removable via quick release connectors to facilitate access to engine; armored cockpit, pressurized cockpit. Entry via starboard opening jettisonable canopy. Braking parachute (_ 4.1m) in tail section
Control Surfaces:	fabric-covered combined elevator-ailerons (elevons) on the outer wing trailing edge with built-in trim tabs. Central vertical stabilizer of wooden construction, fabric covered rudder with integral trim tab
Undercarriage:	retractable tricycle landing gear; main gear retracting upward and aft into the fuselage and nose gear retracting aft into a bulge beneath the nose (also functioning as an emergency skid), retractable tailskid beneath aft fuselage
Engine:	HWK 109-509C with controllable thrust from 400-2,400 kp, with the main engine delivering 400-2,000 kp and the cruise engine 400 kp Several *T-Stoff* tanks in fuselage and *C-Stoff* tanks in the wings with a total capacity of 2,440 liters.
Military Equipment:	2 x MK 108 with 75 rounds of ammunition each in wing roots Revi 16b standard gunsight FuG 16E transmitter/receiver with FuG 16ZE installation kit FuG 25a Identification Friend or Foe

Technical Data

Model		DFS194	Me 163A	Me 163B	Me 163C	Me 263
Dimensions:						
length	m	7.20	5.60	5.70	7.04	7.89
height	m		2.22	2.75	2.75	3.17
Wings:						
span	m	9.30	8.85	9.30	9.80	9.50
sweep %		23.5	23.5	23.5	23.5	
area	m²	17.5	17.5	19.6	20.5	17.8
loading	kg/m²		137	220	248.8	286.5
Weight:						
empty	kg		1,450	1,980	2,200	2,210
takeoff	kg	2,100	2,400	4,310	5,100	5,100
engine		HWK RI-203	HWK RII-203	109-509 A-1	109-509 A-2	109-509C
thrust	kp	400	750	1,600	1,700 + 300	2,000 + 400
Flight performance:						
maximum speed	km/h	550	920	900	950	1,000
landing speed	km/h	120	160	160	160	145
endurance (max. performance)	min		7.5	8	12	15
ceiling	m		10,000	12,000	16,000	16,000
range	km			80	120	200
takeoff run	m		1,200	800		
landing roll	m			600		

Me 163/Me 263 Type Overview:

Me 163A   V4 through V13
Manufacturer: Messerschmitt AG
Engine: HWK RII-203
Armament: none

Me 163 B-0   V1 through V70 preproduction series
Manufacturer: Messerschmitt AG Augsburg and Messerschmitt GmbH Obertraubling
Engine: HWK 109-509 A (RII-211)
Armament: 2 x MG 151/20 (up to and including delivery no. 45);
2 x MK 108 (from delivery no. 46)

Me 163 B-0/R1   lot of 20
Manufacturer: Klemm Company
Engine: HWK 109-509 A-1
Armament: 2 x MK 108

Me 163 B-0/R1   lot of 30, same as B-0/R1 but with reworked wings of the B-1
Manufacturer: Klemm Company
Engine: HWK 109-509 A-1
Armament: 2 x MK 108

Me 163 B-1/R1   lot of 70, forward fuselage section and empennage of the B-0
Manufacturer: Klemm Company
Engine: HWK 109-509B
Armament: 2 x MK 108

Me 163 B-1   lot of 390 planned (main production batch)
Manufacturer: Klemm and Junkers Companies
Engine: HWK 109-509B
Armament: 2 x MK 108

Me 163 B-2   reworked version of B-1
Manufacturer:
Engine: HWK 109-509B
Armament: 2 x MK 108

Me 163 C   four test versions planned, follow-on development of the B-series (raised canopy, longer fuselage and increased wingspan)
Manufacturer: Messerschmitt AG
Engine: HWK 109-509 A-2 (with cruise engine)
Armament: 2 x MK 103 in wing root and 2 x MK 108 in fuselage

Me 163 S   two-seat, unpowered trainer version (conversion of B-series aircraft), lot of 42 planned
Manufacturer: Deutsche Lufthansa
Engine: none
Armament: none

Me 263/Ju 248   three test models built, production series of 972 planned
Manufacturer: Junkers Company
Engine: HWK 109-509 C (with cruise engine)
Armament: 2 x MK 108 in fuselage

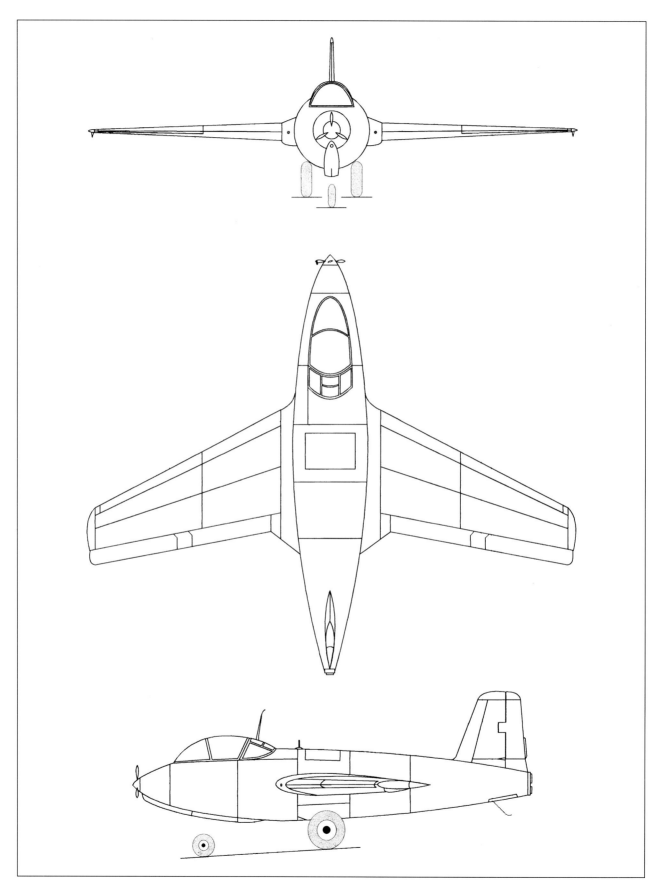

Me 263/Ju 248

Aft section of the Me 263/Ju 348 showing the two rocket exhausts and the braking 'chute pack. (photo: Radinger)

airplanes. To accomplish this task, in November 1944 a comprehensive set of wind tunnel tests were undertaken at Dessau. On 15 December 1944 there was a viewing of an Me 263 mockup at Raguhn. The first test plane, the Me 263 V1, was completed at Dessau by 6 February 1945, in part using a collection of modified new parts and components from the Me 163 B. Pilot Heinz Peters immediately began unpowered flight testing of the type, since a suitable rocket engine was not yet available. A Ju 188 served as the tow plane. Only with the greatest effort was it possible to complete a total of three prototypes (Me 263 V1-V3) by March 1945, although none of these had the rocket engine and were all fitted with a fixed undercarriage. However, it was no longer possible to transfer these planes to JG 400 in Brandis. Particularly since on 20 March 1945 the RLM directed JG 400 to reequip with the He 162 in place of the Me 263.

The Americans were the first to reach Dessau, but after their withdrawal left to the Soviet troops plenty of documents, components, and at least one prototype of the Me 263. This was further evaluated under Soviet supervision. In June 1946 Junkers test pilot Mathis was killed in a crash with the Me 263. A short time later, on 22 October 1946, a large part of the Junkers personnel was shipped to the Soviet Union together with their families under the cover of darkness. There developmental work on the program continued.

Oversight of the Me 263 work was specifically given to the Mikoyan-Gurevich Design Bureau, although this organization actually had pathetically little experience with swept wings and tailless aircraft, which is why its own I-270 and Zh developments (undoubtedly strongly influenced by the Me 263) made use of straight wings and a T-tail. However, after the two prototypes built crashed, the program was canceled.

Japanese Variants

With the American B-29 raids on Japan and a demonstration of German jet aircraft for Japanese delegates in Rechlin, Japan showed a strong interest in the two new German types, the Me 163 and the Me 262. Ultimately, export of these two weapons systems was cleared at the highest level of government. In April 1944 the RLM held a conference on the subject where, among other things, it outlined the issuance of a license to Japan for the manufacture of the Me 163 B, the Me 262 A-1, the Jumo 004 jet engine, the HWK 109-509 rocket engine, and the production of special fuels. That same year the first technical documents were sent to Japan via submarine. It is, however, un-

Japanese variant of the Me 163 B, the Mitsubishi J8M1. *Shusui*

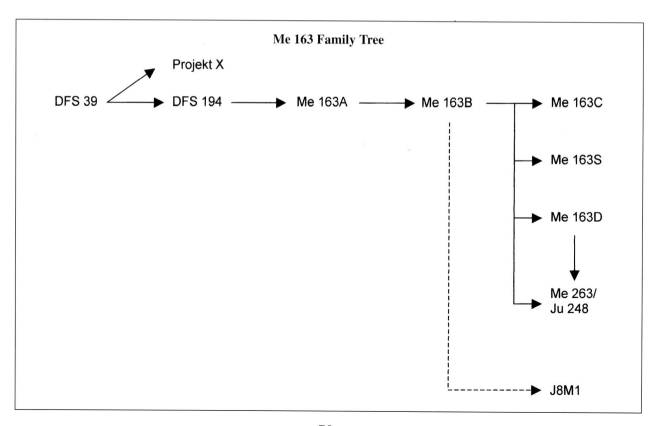

known whether the sub ever made it to its destination. The license contract itself was signed with Japan in December 1944. Following this, a further two submarines left Kiel in January 1945 with production plans for the Me 163 B and Me 262, as well as critical components and equipment for the two types. One of the two subs was sunk in the Atlantic. The second submarine was forced to dock at a submarine base in Norway in order to carry out repairs. It sailed again in March 1945 and surrendered at sea when the war ended.

Nevertheless, using the scanty documents available the Japanese succeeded in copying (in modified form) both the Me 262 (as the Nakajima J8N1) as well as the Me 163, and flew both types by August 1945.

The Mitsubishi Jukogyo KK company was contracted for license manufacture of the Me 163. The type was designated J8M1 *Shusui*, which roughly translated means "powerful sword." The first model of the airplane was completed in September 1944, following which a developmental contract was issued. In conjunction with this, a contract was also drawn up for the construction of an unpowered glider version of the J8M1 for pilot training. This training variant carried the designation MXY7 *Akigusa* (Autumn Grass); the first trainer version was completed by mid-December 1944. The aviation development center in Yoko Suzuka carried out license manufacture of the Walter HWK 109-509 A rocket engine under the designation *Toku Ro 2*. The first prototype of the J8M1 was finished by June 1945. That same month the first *Toku Ro 2* engine arrived at Mitsubishi and was incorporated into the aircraft in early July 1945.

The first rocket-powered takeoff of the J8M1 took place on 7 July 1945, ending in a crash when the *Toku Ro 2* engine suddenly shut down of its own accord at an altitude of 400 meters.

Two additional prototypes were built, but no further flights were ever carried out.

Postwar Allied Testing

The western Allies acquired a total of 48 intact Me 163s, of which 19 were destroyed by German troops. Four planes went to France and a further 25 to England, with ultimately two eventually making their way to the United States.

The Soviet Union captured an unknown number of Me 163s, but at least one of these was a flight-ready Me 163 B and an Me 163S.

The British aircraft carrier *HMS Reaper* ferried captured German aircraft from Cherbourg, France, to Newark, New Jersey, after the war. Numbered among these were two Me 163 Bs. From there the airplanes were transported by rail to Freeman Field in Indiana, where they arrived on 10 August 1945. A test program was drawn up for the Me 163 B—now designated FE500 (*WerkNr.* 191301)—on 5 October 1945 and approved on 31 October of that year. The second *Komet* was to become part of a touring exhibition.

The first *Komet* was completely overhauled by 21 March 1946, including a replacement of the original wings with those from Me 163 B *WerkNr.* 191190. On 12 April 1946 the airplane was transported via a C-82 to Muroc AFB (today's Edwards AFB). The associated personnel, which included Dr. Alexander Lippisch, were not sent to Muroc until 30 April 1946. Upon arriving at Muroc AFB Dr. Lippisch adjudged the Me 1263B to be in very poor condition. Nevertheless, on 3 May 1946 an attempt was made for a towed flight behind a B-29, although this failed due to complications with the release mechanism. Because of the many technical problems and serious difficulties in obtaining spare parts the U.S. was unable to carry out a test program with the Me 163 B, neither as a glider, nor using its rocket engine.

From 1946 onward England focused on a supersonic project with a planned speed of Mach 1.24 at 11,000 meters' altitude. Involved in this project were the Germans Dr. Multhopp (formerly director of advanced project studies with Focke-Wulf) and Dr. Winter (wind tunnel expert at the AVA Göttingen).

The aircraft's design included a wing sweep of a remarkable 55 degrees. The pilot was to lie prone beneath the intake for the Rolls Royce Avon engine. Landing would be made on a shock absorbing skid, calculated at a speed of 257 km/h. In order to gain experience with this landing method at this speed range, up until 15 November 1947 the Royal Aircraft Establishment (RAE) used the Me 163 B with the RAE designation VF 241 for research into high speed skid landings. After the familiarization phase with the plane was completed, the actual high speed landing test phase began on 13 November 1947 at RAF Wittering, a former Allied satellite airfield for recovering crippled bombers. This phase involved gradually—by means of landing flaps—increasing the landing speed up to 254 km/h, a speed which lengthened the rollout to 560 meters. During a flight on 15 November 1947 the support brace of the skid broke on touchdown and pushed up into the fuselage. The control rods became bent and the cockpit was completely wrecked.

Because the British viewed the *T*- and *C-Stoff* special fuels as extremely dangerous and not yet matured, the Me 163 B was never flown in England under its own power—there was no desire to jeopardize the lives of British test pilots. As earlier described, the Soviet Union made use of their test results with the Me 163/Me 263 in its MiG Zh and I-270 programs which, however, were soon canceled. A large percentage of the captured airplanes were scrapped a few years after the war once the Allies' interest in this plane dropped. Throughout the world today there are at least 10 Me 163s in museums, exhibits, and collections.

In Germany itself there are currently two Me 163 Bs. One plane was given by British Air Commodore R. Deacon Elliot to a German delegation at the former British fighter base of Biggen Hill in Kent on 28 November 1964. The airplane was transported to Germany and subsequently given a thorough overhaul at the Messerschmitt Works at Manching (near Ingolstadt). Since 1965 this airplane can be viewed as part of the aviation exhibit in the Deutsches Museum in Munich. The second machine (*WerkNr.* 191904 of JG 400) was handed over by the RAF to the *Bundesluftwaffe* on 5 May 1988 and can now be seen at the *Luftwaffenmuseum* in Berlin Gatow. Additional airplanes are located at:

Me 163 B (with RAF identification AM 210) during an exhibition at West Raynham.

- the Science Museum, London
- the Imperial War Museum, Duxford (near Cambridge)
- RAF Cosford Aeropsace Museum, Birmingham
- Museum of Flight, East Fortune (Scotland)
- National Air and Space Museum, Washington (stored in the Smithsonian Institution's warehouses at Silver Hill, Maryland)
- War Memorial Museum, Canberra (in storage)

Me 163 B (*Werk-Nr.* 191904) at the museum in Colerne, before it was returned to the *Bundeswehr Luftwaffe*.

This page: Me 163 B (*Werk-Nr.* 191904) exhibited at the *Luftwaffe* museum in Berlin-Gatow.

74

Me 163 B (*Werk-Nr. 191659*), with the "T" and "C" annotations on the fuselage spine clearly labeled.

Me 163 B with RAF markings of VF 241.

Messerschmitt Me 262 Interceptor

Compared to the Allied piston-engined fighters, the Me 262 demonstrated markedly superior flight handling, but because of its long takeoff run it was precisely at this stage that it was extremely vulnerable to low-flying enemy fighters. This led to Me 109s and Fw 190s patrolling the skies over the Me 262 operational squadrons' airfields to protect them from strafing enemy fighters.

It was for this reason that *Erprobungskommando 262* at Lechfeld, together with the Karlshagen test center, through October 1944 carried out comprehensive trials of the Rheinmetall-Borsig RI-502 (1,000 kp thrust) solid fuel booster rockets. These solid fuel booster rockets were attached near the aft fuel tank hatch beneath the fuselage. This dramatically improved takeoff performance, thereby reducing the takeoff run. In January 1945 *Kommando Stamp* (testing bombardment of enemy bomber formations) in Lärz carried out trials with the more powerful Rheinmetall-Borsig RI-503 solid fuel rocket. This booster rocket developed a rated thrust of 1,000 kp and a maximum thrust of 3,000 kp, weighing a total of 100 kg. The experiments, however, were broken off due to unsatisfactory results.

For the reasons described above, as early as 1943 Messerschmitt began thinking about fitting the Me 262 with a supplemental rocket motor. This would have the advantage of offering both a rapidly climbing point defense fighter, as well as providing extended operating time for a pursuit fighter. In late July 1943 three concept proposals for an Me 262 interceptor were drawn up under the direction of Messrs. Degel and Althoff:

Above left: Me 262 A-1a (V1+AC) as a testbed for rocket-assisted takeoff.

Above: Solid-fuel RI-502 rockets.

Above right: Cockpit control panel for rocket-assisted takeoff. (photos: Radinger)

- Interceptor 1 with 2 x Jumo 004C and an additional 1 x HWK 109-509S; armament 6 x MK 108
- Interceptor II with 2 x BMW 003R engines; armament 6 x MK 108
- Interceptor III with 2 x HWK 109-509 A-2; armament 6 x MK 108

Me 262C-1a (Interceptor I)

The first draft of the Interceptor I was completed by 26 May 1943. This was an Me 262 A-1a with two Jumo 004C turbojet engines, supplemented by an HWK 109-509S rocket propulsion system. The fuel system would consist of three tank groups, permitting the following quantities to be carried:

J2 fuel: 900 liters
T-Stoff: 900 liters
C-Stoff: 400 liters

The design bureau estimated the performance of this Me 262C-1a to be:

maximum speed:	950 km/h
climb to 10,000 m:	2.8 min
endurance:	26 min. max
range:	300 km max

The first project description of this Me 262C-1a was submitted with the date of 11 October 1943. It included plans for fitting an acid-resistant tank system. In addition, the undercarriage would be strengthened in view of the higher takeoff weight, plus the armament would be increased to 6 x MK 108 cannons, giving this type a much greater punch compared to the standard Me 262 A-1a.

By July 1943 there began preparations for converting the Me 262 A-1a to the specifications of the C-1a. But it was not until 2 September 1944 that the actual

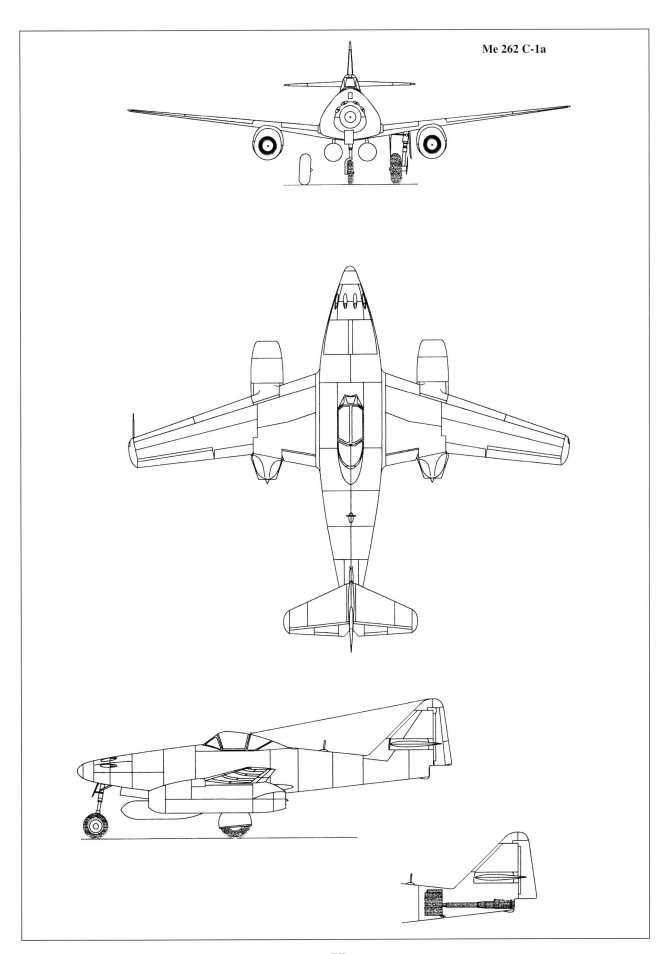

Me 262 C-1a

Me 262-V186 as the testbed for the Me 262 C-1a, seen during takeoff with the rocket motor switched on. (photo: Radinger)

conversion work began on Me 262 A-1a (*WerkNr.* 130 186) at the Oberbayerische Forschungsanstalt in Oberammergau. This facility was a remote test center for the Messerschmitt AG. Conversion included installing an HWK 109-509S rocket system with 1,700 kp thrust into the tail of the airplane, and involved extensive modification to the fuel system for accepting the rocket fuel. The vertical stabilizer also had to be shortened to prevent it from protruding into the hot exhaust gases of the rocket motor. Work was finished in late October 1944, and the *Organisation Todt* transported the airplane by road from Oberammergau to Lagerlechfeld. There the aircraft was reassembled and flown three times using jet power alone for checking out and accepting the airplane.

On 25 October 1944 the first ground runs were carried out using the installed Walter engine, which resulted in changes being made to the engine mount. In November 1944 there were often interruptions in the work due to the increasing number of air raids against Lechfeld and the poor weather that month. On 18 December 1944 another ground run was conducted with the rocket engine, but again there was a crack in a welded seam within the combustion chamber. The chamber was swapped out, but on the next ground run in mid-January 1945 the engine caught fire due to an

improper seal. The combustion chamber was again exchanged for a new one, and on 27 February 1945 Gerd Lindner took off with the rocket motor switched on for the first rocket/jet powered flight. On this flight he reached an altitude of 8,000 meters within the space of three minutes. Subsequently there were six additional takeoffs with the Me 262, now bearing the markings of V186. Because of damage to the nose gear during a test flight the plane was parked in a revetment for repairs. But the V186 was seriously damaged during a nighttime low-level attack against Lechfeld on 23 March 1945. Although the Messerschmitt Company repaired the testbed, it had not been fully reassembled by the time the war ended.

After the Allies occupied Lagerlechfeld the V186 was transported to the Royal Aircraft Establishment at Farnborough, where it was examined in detail before eventually being scrapped.

Me 262C-2b Interceptor II

BMW first proposed the idea of a BMW 003 turbojet engine with a liquid fuel rocket motor mounted on top in the summer of 1942. The first successful bench test of a complete BMW 003R TLR took place in March 1944 at the BMW Works in Berlin Spandau. TLR was the designation for the combined turbojet and rocket

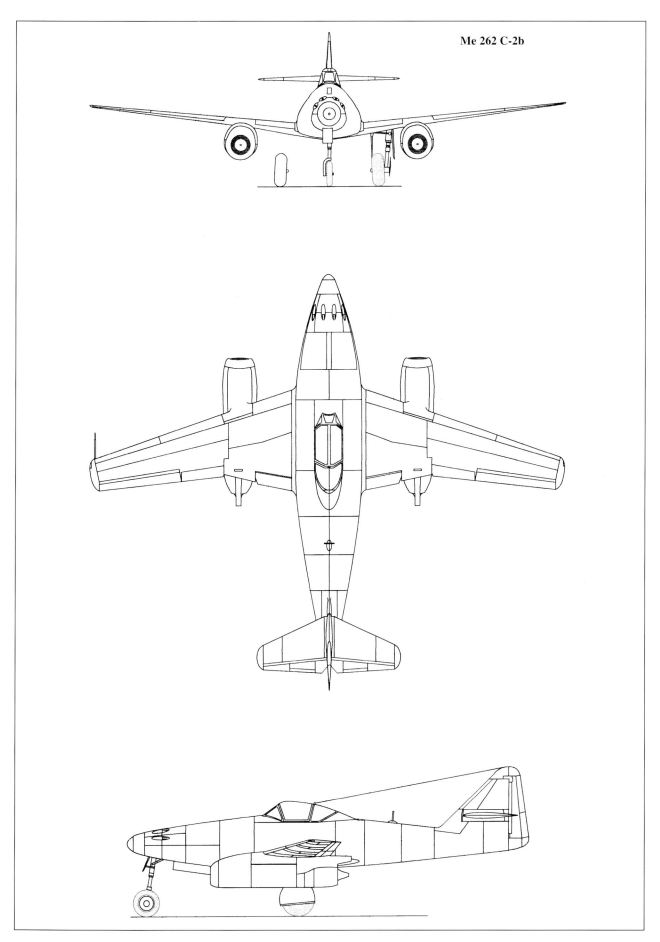

Me 262 C-2b

Above: Me 262-V074 as the testbed for the *Interceptor II*. Below: Static run-up of the rocket engine on the Me 262-V074. (photos: Radinger)

The Messerschmitt design bureau calculated the following performance data for the Me 262 C-3:

takeoff weight:	5,480 kg	
climb rate	to 12,000 m	2 min 26 sec (including takeoff and landing)
	to 16,000 m	3 min 4 sec (including takeoff and landing)
endurance:	at 12,000 m	7 min 36 sec (at 800 km/h)
	at 16,000 m	4 min 30 sec (at 800 km/h)
range:		270 to 310 km

engines. The concept was taken up by Messerschmitt in developing the Me 262 Interceptor II concept. The airplane was to have been fitted with two BMW 003A-1 turbojet engines, with a BMW 109-718 rocket engine being fitted to the top of each of these. This gave a total thrust per engine of 2,050 kmp, with 800 kp being provided by the turbine and 1,250 kp by the rocket motor.

In accordance with the Messerschmitt terminology for designating Me 262 variants this version was designated Me 262C-2b. A concept proposal for modifying a normal Me 262 A-2b to an Me 262C-2b was submitted by Messerschmitt on 1 September 1943. The conversion included the installation of a corrosion-resistant special fuel system, strengthened landing gear, and additional jettisonable fuel tanks for increasing the operating time from 50 to 70 minutes. In addition, like the Interceptor I the armament was increased to 6 x MK 108.

In October 1943 BMW was contracted to supply a total of 15 BMW 003R TLR engines by June 1944.

In early 1944 Messerschmitt began design work for the conversion measures. Testbed was to be an Me 262 with the *Werknummer* 170074. Conversion of the airplane also took place at the test construction center within the Oberbayerische Forschungsanstalt in Oberammergau.

The V074, as the test plane was then officially designated, was transported by road to Lagerlechfeld, where it arrived on 20 December 1944. The airplane was reassembled, and on 8 January 1945 a flight under pure turbojet power was conducted. Yet later there were again sealant problems with the TLR engines, as the seals used were not resistant enough against the aggressive rocket fuel. In addition, there were delivery problems with replacement parts and rocket fuel. It was not until 23 March 1945 that a satisfactory ground run with the two TLR propulsion systems could finally be carried out.

On 26 March 1945 *Flugkapitän* Baur took off in the V074 on the first flight with rocket motors switched on. The flight and subsequent landing ran without a problem. Baur reached an altitude of 8,200 meters in 1.5 minutes, with the two rocket motors burning 40 seconds each during that time. Just three days later the second flight with TLR propulsion took place, during the course of which problems with one of the rocket engines occurred. After that, it was no longer possible to carry out testing with the V074, since the B4 fuel needed for the two BMW turbojet engines could no longer be supplied. In these final days of the war there was no chance to convert the jet engines to J2 fuel, as used by the Jumo 004 engines from the outset. The Me 262C-2b was parked at Lagerlechfeld. Thus ended the story of the Interceptor II, in just as unspectacular a fashion as that of the Interceptor I.

Interceptor III

A more radical path was pursued in designing the Interceptor III. The two turbojets were to have been replaced by two HWK 109-509 A-2 rocket system, each with 1,700 kp thrust, in order to provide a purebred point defense fighter.

In September 1944 Messerschmitt drew up plans for converting an Me 262 A-2 to the Me 262 C-3, as the Me 262 Interceptor III was designated. In addition to swapping out the engines, this would involve the modification of the fuel tank system (fuel tanks made of anti-corrosive metals), the use of jettisonable fuel tanks for increasing the endurance of the plane, and arming the aircraft with 6 x MK 108 cannons.

But this purebred rocket fighter version of the Me 262 met with little interest within the RLM, chiefly because the Me 163 B was already tagged for operations as a point defense fighter. Plus, as far as the RLM was concerned, at this time there was a greater need for markedly better performing and simpler to produce "disposable planes," as exemplified by the design of a Bachem *Natter*. Not to be forgotten were the countless numbers of ultra-small rocket fighter designs that matured within the individual aviation companies from late 1944 onward.

Ernst Bachem

Bachem Ba 349 *Natter*

Dipl.Ing. Erich Bachem was the technical director at the Fieseler Works in Kassel, went independent, and set up a small aviation supplier company in Bad Waldsee (Württemberg). With 1943/1944's backdrop of incessant heavy American bomber daylight raids and their accompanying escort fighters, in the summer of 1944 Erich Bachem and Willy Fiedler began develop-

ing the concept of a high speed and easily produced defense plane that could reach high altitudes in the shortest time under VFR conditions and be operated with the minimum of training. This "manned rocket," purely for point defense, would be stationed immediately adjacent to the site requiring protection and would not be launched until the Allied bomber formations had been sighted. In his concept study, Bachem also took the following into account:

Bachem Ba 349 with the perfect complement of 24 *Föhn* rockets. (*Bundesarchiv*)

- forward armor protection for the pilot
- simplified construction
- where possible, built of wood to save iron
- use of the wood industry's extensive and partially untapped resources
- no strain on the normal aviation industry
- multiple use of critical components (airframe and engine parts)

It was Erich Bachem's good fortune that, in the late summer of 1944, the RLM issued a requirement for a cheap defensive fighter ("disposable plane"). This airplane was expected to be able to take off when enemy bomber formations were in visible range and intercept them before they reached their intended target.

This requirement necessitated the use of rocket propulsion.

A total of four companies submitted design proposals. Although Erich Bachem was not officially a participant in the request for tender, he submitted his proposal unsolicited nevertheless. The companies and their projects were:

Heinkel	Project P.1077 *Julia*
Junkers	EF 127 *Wally*
Messerschmitt	Me P.1104
Bachem	BP20

The RLM selected Erich Bachem's proposal, and in September 1944 it issued a contract for the produc-

Bachem Ba 349 showing the rocket tubes and the sighting mechanism. (*Deutsches Museum* Munich)

83

tion of 15 prototypes to be built at Bad Waldsee. The program also called for wind tunnel experiments with the BP20 at the DVL in Berlin-Adlershof and in Braunschweig. To this end, in January 1945 a 1/2.5 scale wooden model of the BP20 was brought to Berlin and, beginning on 30 January 1945, underwent wind tunnel testing. It is extremely doubtful that the results of these tests ever made it back to the Bachem Company in their entirety.

At the same time, the venture was entered into the emergency fighter program under the number 8-349.

The BP20 was a remarkably unusual design compared to the other proposals submitted. It clearly reflected the BP20's envisioned role. The aircraft was to take off vertically, and to that end was equipped with four Schmidding 500 kp thrust solid fuel rockets (or two SG 34 solid fuel rockets with 1,000 kp thrust each) in addition to the main engine. The booster rockets were affixed to the aft fuselage. These solid fuel rock-

ets, however, suffered from a certain tolerance (incurred by the production technology of the day) with regard to the direction of thrust, thus the line of force, making a precise alignment of the boosters particularly difficult. It was therefore planned to make use of a vertical frame for launching the airplane that would direct the aircraft during the initial stage of takeoff. This frame also enabled the airplane to operate independent of fixed airfields. The burned out booster rockets would be jettisoned approximately 10 seconds after launch, at an altitude of about 1,000 meters. The internal main engine would then propel the aircraft to the bombers' operating altitude of about 9,000 meters. Because of the rocket engine's short burn time the pilot would then have to immediately engage the enemy aircraft and fire his unguided air-to-air rockets carried in the nose. He would then break off engagement in a steep dive, pulling up and bleeding off speed once sufficient distance had separated him from the enemy

Bachem Ba 349A on the launch rail.

84

Bachem Ba 349A on the launch rail, with the ignition line being attached. (*Deutsches Museum* Munich)

planes. This allowed the automatic separation of the nose section from the rest of the fuselage. Once the two fuselage sections separated, the pilot and important equipment components (e.g. instrument panel) would be extracted via the main parachute from the nose section. The aft part of the fuselage would drift down to earth on a parachute located in a box on the starboard side for recovery of the rocket system and the control surfaces. This unorthodox method of "landing" was chosen because of the dangers inherent in the rocket fuel, particularly the high risk of explosion on landing.

In October 1944 Bachem issued its initial manufacturing sheet for its airplane, now officially known as the Ba 349 (derived from the RLM's designation 8-349).

In November 1944 the RLM took a critical look at the Ba 349's armament. At first two MK 108 cannons in the nose, each with 30 rounds, was consid-

ered. This meant, however, that the two cannons would be lost after every operational mission flown, as they would fall to earth with the disposable nose section. As a result, the *Rohrbatterie 108* was scrutinized. This was a 32 tube weapon, each tube containing a single projectile. The disadvantage of these projectiles was their extremely limited range of just 350 meters. Other armament that was considered included 24 Hs 217 *Föhn* rockets and 33 R4M rockets.

The Hs 217 *Föhn* rocket was an unguided solid fuel (piglycol) weapon with a caliber of 7.3 cm. It was originally conceived as a ground-to-air weapon, and with its range of 1,200 meters was designed for use against low-flying Allied fighters. The projectile had a weight of 3 kg. Production began in October 1944 as part of the 1944/45 emergency anti-aircraft program (*Flak-Notprogramm 1944/45*)

The R4M *Orkan* by Rheinmetall was a fin-stabilized unguided solid fuel (diglycol) rocket with a cali-

Bachem Ba 349A on the launch rail. (*Deutsches Museum* Munich)

ber of 5.5. cm. In the designation R4M, the R stood for "rocket," the 4 indicated the projectile's weight of 4 kg, and the M stood for "mine warhead" (.5 kg explosive charge). The rocket reached a maximum velocity of 900 km/s and had a range of 1,800 meters. All told, about 12,000 of these remarkably successful rockets were produced during the final months of the war. The RLM felt that the primary role of the Ba 349 was to engage heavily armed bombers, such as the B-17 and B-24.

With a date of 27 November 1944 Bachem submitted a project description of the Ba 349 together with a deadline plan for the program. According to this plan, development would run from September 1944 to January 1945, by which time 50 prototypes would be completed. Testing of these prototypes would be finished by the end of February 1945. Manufacture of the pre-production batch (totaling 200 aircraft) would begin as early as January 1945 and conclude by the end of March 1945. Testing of the pre-production series was expected to stretch from February to April 1945. Full scale production would start in mid-February 1945, with an expected output of production planes by March 1945. Parallel to these plans, development and testing of the trainers would run from December 1944 to February 1945, with training of pilots expected to get underway by early March 1945. Of the 50 prototypes, 10 each would be used for testing in the following areas:

- flight handling evaluation
- research into vertical takeoff
- solution to problems of saving the pilot and recovering the aircraft
- experiments with installed control systems
- overall design testing

The first manned vertical takeoff was planned for airplane no. 51. The actual course of testing, however, deviated considerably from these plans.

Prototypes M1 through M6 were used for evaluating the flight handling characteristics of the design and were towed behind an He 111H-6(DG+RN). The M1 prototype had no undercarriage, but made use of a provisional takeoff trolley made of a tubular steel frame with two main wheels and a swiveling nose wheel attached to it. Aircraft M2 and M3 were fitted with their own fixed landing gear. These made use of the main wheels from a Klemm Kl 35 attached to the wings and a nose wheel located beneath the forward separation bulkhead. None of these aircraft had a rocket engine installed. The tow cables were latched onto the two wingtips. A parachute was fitted into the aft section of the airplanes's fuselages. Testing of the aircraft took place at the airfield at Neuburg, on the Danube. The planes were towed to altitude and then tested in a glide after cable release. These tests included attaining altitudes of up to 5,500 meters and achieving speeds of up to 700 km/h during the subsequent glide. The airplane exhibited surprisingly good stability throughout.

The first prototypes had a canopy that opened to the right. During separation testing at Ainring, with follow-on separation of the nose and recovery of the fuselage using the internal parachute, it was discovered that the canopy would jam shut due to its side hinge. The remainder of the aircraft, therefore, were fitted with a rear opening canopy. This had the added advantage of ensuring the canopy would automatically break away with the force of the slipstream after opening.

The next airplanes would test the vertical takeoff system. Because of a shortage of HWK rocket engines, takeoff was to be made using only the solid fuel booster rockets, which simultaneously limited the potential altitude that could be reached. On 19 December 1944 the first airplane (probably the M7) was fitted with four booster rockets and set up on a launch tower on top of the Heuberg, near Hechingen. The solid fuel rockets had undergone thorough bench testing in various configurations beforehand. They were ignited, and after a second the aircraft would break free of its retainers. But it never lifted off; instead, it caught fire and became consumed in flames. As was discovered later, the release cable for the retainers had simply burned up due to the enormous heat. Changes were made, and subsequent testing revealed no further problems. The first successful vertical launch of a Ba 349 from a tower occurred four days later, on 22 December 1944. The airplane climbed smoothly up to an altitude of about 800 meters. These vertical takeoff trials served as a basis for researching the airplane's climb characteristics, its travel up the rail tower, the initial flight path, and examining pilot rescue options. Such unmanned launches were carried out using a total of 10 prototypes. Very soon, though, they revealed problems with the solid fuel rocket motors. The rockets' line of thrust could vary up to 0.5 degrees from the intended direction. By using four rockets the problem either corrected itself or compounded itself, which could lead to major course deviations. For later vertical takeoffs a fix was found by attaching control vanes in the exhaust stream of the main engine (on those aircraft having an internal engine). These vanes were controlled automatically by a Patin 3-axis autostabilizer, which also controlled the shift from vertical to horizontal flight. The control vanes were kept cool during the solid fuel rockets' burn time by jets of water, but afterwards they simply burned away, as they were no longer needed. Correcting the deviations in the booster rockets' direction of thrust using the aircraft's normal control surfaces was not possible, because the airflow over the surfaces was too low in the initial stage of launch. A further problem illuminated by these early takeoff trials was a pronounced shift in the center of gravity caused by jettisoning the burned out booster rockets, which in turn led to stability problems. A fix was made by using extensions to enlarge the surface of the elevators by 1.0 m², increasing the span of the horizontal stabilizers to 4.5 meters. These extensions were jettisoned together with the solid fuel boosters. Because of the urgency of the program there were many mishaps during the testing program, each one of which resulted in the loss of the aircraft.

As part of this vertical takeoff testing program, there were also studies made with launch towers of different heights to determine the necessary minimum frame length. The first planes were launched with a frame 17.0 meters long. A 12.5 meter frame was then tried before an 8 meter frame was settled upon, at least for testing purposes (later operational missions were to have made use of a 9 meter frame). The following paragraphs offer brief examples of the launches of four prototypes.

Aircraft M16 was launched from a 17 meter frame. But the solid fuel boosters only delivered 990 kp instead of the required 1,200 kp of thrust. This meant that the initial velocity of the aircraft upon leaving the launch tower was just 18 meters per second. Furthermore, upon exiting the frame, severe thrust oscillations began building up. The rockets burned out after 10 seconds. It was later determined that one of the boosters did not fully burn.

Prototype M17 took off from the 12.5 meter frame. Here, too, the engines at 815 kp did not deliver the needed thrust. The airplane climbed to an altitude of

2,500 meters instead of the planned 3,750 meters. With the launch of M31 from an 8 meter frame one of the rocket nozzles broke off. The resulting asymmetrical thrust caused the aircraft to rotate 90 degrees on its longitudinal axis and then climb upward at a 45 degree angle. M32 made use of trim tabs. After leaving the launch tower, the airplane rotated 22 degrees on its longitudinal axis and then climbed in a vertical line.

With the bombing of the Schmidding Works in Bodenbach in February 1945 there were no longer any solid fuel booster rockets to be had. The time was filled by increasing the tempo of Ba 349 towed flights behind He 111s at Neuburg. Vertical takeoff experiments were able to resume at the end of February.

It was also in February 1945 that the HWK engines were finally made available, and on 25 February the first unmanned takeoff of a complete aircraft took place. All phases of the flight, to include landing, went smoothly. The pilot was simulated by a dummy.

Based on this, the SS High Command (which had assumed oversight of the program in the interim) ordered the immediate execution of a manned launch for the month of February, something that had originally been planned for aircraft no. 51. *Olt* Siebert volunteered to be the pilot, and on 1 March everything was ready. Launch of the M23 went without a problem. The aircraft climbed normally, but then rolled over onto its back at a 30 degree angle before disappearing into the clouds seconds later. When the airplane again appeared in view, it was in a steep dive and impacted the ground shortly thereafter. Investigation later revealed that the canopy probably broke away during the climb out. The pilot's headrest was also attached to the canopy, which meant that *Olt* Siebert was either immediately rendered unconscious or suffered a broken neck. This explained why fuselage, pilot, and nose did not separate at altitude, resulting in the entire airplane crashing at the end of an uncontrolled dive. The airplane's rotation onto its back and the 30 degree climb angle were traced back to one of two causes:

Technical Data					
		M16	M17	M31	M32
takeoff weight	kg	1,630	1,610	1,610	1,610
wing area	m²	3.6	3.6	3.6	3.6
wing chord	m	1.0	1.0	1.0	1.0
theoretical thrust	kp	4 x 1,200	4 x 1,200	4 x 1,200	4 x 1,200
actual thrust	kp	4 x 990	4 x 980-815		
burn time	s	10	10-12		
altitude	m	770	2,500		
launch tower length	m	17.0	12,5	8.0	8.0

Bachem Ba 349

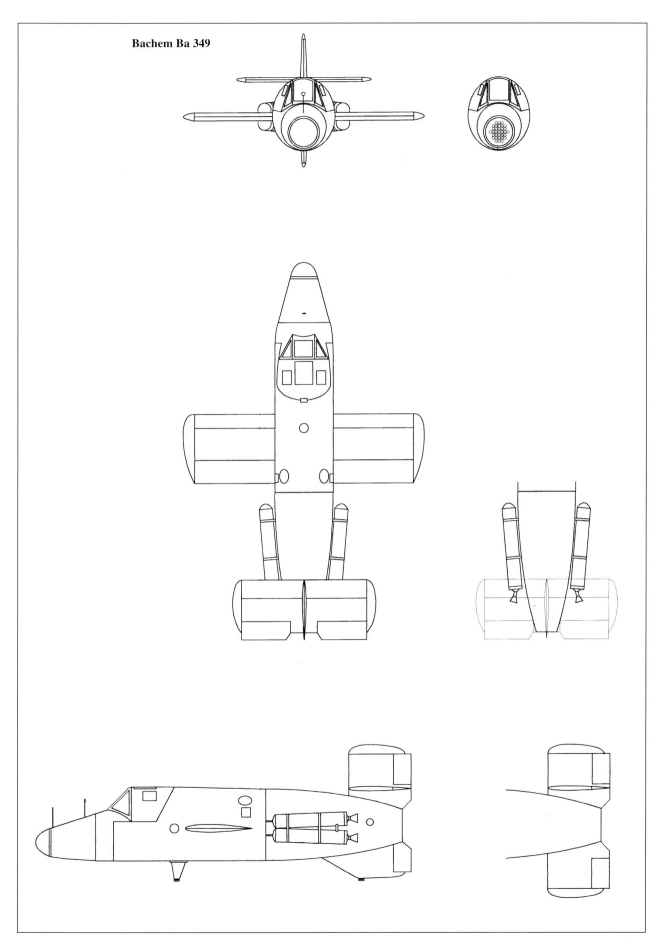

either fluttering control vanes in the HWK engine's exhaust, or incorrectly adjusted solid fuel boosters.

Experiments with unmanned aircraft continued through April 1945. A total of 18 unmanned flights were carried out. Many sources claim that additional manned flights were conducted, and although this cannot be determined with any certainty, with today's perspective it is highly unlikely in view of the circumstances during the final stages of the war, particularly as special fuels and replacement parts became increasingly difficult to acquire. The experiments carried out showed that, counter to intended operational plans, the aft fuselage could not be reused—it invariably exploded on contact with the ground because of the fuel remaining in the tanks.

Manufacture of the pre-production lot began even as the test program was ongoing. Production was distributed out to several different sites in order to minimize the impact of any air raids. The estimated expenditure of a production aircraft to delivery amounted to just 600 man hours. Final assembly would take place at the Bachem Works in Bad Waldsee or at the Hirth Works at Teck/Nabern (which had been given a contract for 10). Shortly before the war's end part of the production moved from Bad Waldsee to St. Leonhart, in Austria.

Although the airframe was made entirely of wood, certain high-value components were also needed, for example:

- rocket engine
- engine regulator (throttle)
- armament (only in the event if equipped with the MK 108)
- Patin 3-axis autostabilizer
- cockpit instruments
- oxygen system

which of necessity would lead to bottlenecks in delivery. The following procedures were drawn up for operations with the production version:

1. As soon as enemy bomber formation is sighted the direction post acquires the target, and the pilot simultaneously activates the on-board electronics system
2. The launch tower's ground crew sets the angle and then clears the area.
3. The pilot applies full throttle and checks the controls.
4. The pilot holds on to the side handles and pushes the start button.
5. Takeoff is fully automatic (not least due to the extremely intense acoustic load), either from the launch frame or from a three point tether. The break-free velocity is 90 km/h, at which point the rockets' propulsion has stabilized.
6. Takeoff is enhanced by four jettisonable Schmidding SG34 booster rockets, each with 1,200 kp of thrust.
7. Approach to the enemy formation is accomplished by a "dog's turn" (remotely guided technique in which the speed vector of the aircraft is constantly directed toward the target). This is done to relieve the pilot and to stabilize the launch procedure automatically, and involves the use of the K23 fighter direction control.
8. Final approach to the target is done manually from below at an angle of 15 degrees. At a distance of 500 to 1,000 meters the on-board rockets are fired at corresponding intervals.
9. Additional attacks may continue as long as rockets are available and the altitude remains under 10,000 meters.

Ba 349 Type Overview	
Ba 349A	per the project description of 27 November 1944. RLM series designation was 8-349, from which was ultimately derived the Ba 349 designation. A large number of the prototypes built under contract were produced under this designation, with the majority lacking the main engine, however.
Ba 349B	taller and longer fuselage compared to the A-series to accommodate increased fuel capacity and resulting extended range.
Ba 349C	wings moved aft and made detachable to facilitate ease of transportation. In addition, the elevators moved higher up on the vertical stabilizer (as had been tested earlier in the DVL wind tunnel) *Schulnatter* the idea of modifying a twin engined propeller driven aircraft into a *Schulnatter* trainer. This was to have a *Natter* cockpit fitted into the aircraft in such a manner that the student pilot could steer the plane into the target using supplemental controls. Takeoff and landing would not be taught, since these were superfluous in light of the *Natter's* operational profile.

10. Break off attack by diving away from the enemy, then reduce speed by pulling up.
11. The pilot unbuckles himself, then removes the control stick. The forward fuselage section is blown free and the parachute deploys.
12. The pilot frees himself from the aft fuselage section and at a safe altitude deploys his seat parachute.

In all, a total of 36 Bachem Ba 349 *Natters* were built before the war ended, of which 22 aircraft were used for testing. Ten airplanes were destroyed in testing by the war's end. U.S. troops captured three intact Ba 349s, and the Soviets also found an intact Ba 349 at a satellite branch of the Hirth Company in Thuringia. In addition to four burned out Ba 349s at Bad Waldsee and two more at Ötztal, American forces also reputedly discovered several partially completed aircraft from the pre-production series.

A restored Ba 349 is currently located in the *DeutschesMuseum* in Munich.

Ba 349 Weight Distribution with 2 x MK 108	
(as of 27 November 1944)	
nose section	17 kg
fuselage center section with wings	117 kg
fuselage aft section	30 kg
empennage	59 kg
control surfaces	25 kg
autopilot	35 kg
tanks	43 kg
instruments	6 kg
engine	170 kg
pilot seat	4 kg
armored glass plate	25 kg
armor plating	139 kg
battery	25 kg
recovery parachutes	80 kg
armament and ammunition	185 kg
pilot 100 kg	
fuel	750 kg
RATO booster pods (4 units)	460 kg
takeoff weight	**2,270 kg**

Bachem Ba 349A on the launch rail. (*Deutsches Museum* **Munich)**

Ba 349 Technical Data (as of Oct/Nov 1944)

Type		Ba 349A	Ba 349B	Ba 349C
wings				
span	m	3.6	4.0	-
area	m²	3.6	4.7	-
chord	m	1.0	1.2	-
aspect ratio		3.6	3.4	-
thickness	%	12	12	-
wing loading				
full	kg/m²	453	568	-
empty	kg/m²	222	233	-
length	m	5.72	6.02	-
height	m	2.2	2.225	
fuselage height	m	1.17	1.3	-
fuselage width	m	0.9	0.9	-
horizontal stabilizers				
span	m	2.3	2.4	-
area	m²	2.3	2.4	-
chord	m	1.0	1.0	-
control surface chord	%	35	35	-
vertical stabilizer				
area	m²	2.25	2.25	-
control surface chord	%	30	30	-
rudder area	m²	0.31	0.31	-
fuels				
total weight	kg	600	750	-
T-Stoff	l	365	400	450
C-Stoff	l	165	190	195
Engine		HWK 109-509 A-2	HWK 109-509 A-2	HWK 109-509
Thrust	kp	150-1700	150-1700	150-1700
spec. consumption (max. thrust)	g/kps	3.2	3.2	-
spec. consumption (cruise)	g/kps	6	6	-
RATO boosters		2 x SG34	4 x SG34	4 x SG34
thrust	kp	2 x 1,200	4 x 1,200	4 x 1,200
weight	kg	230	460	460
weight empty	kg	800	1,095	-
takeoff weight	kg	1,630-2,050	2,270	2,050
armament		24 x Föhn	24 x Föhn	-
		33 x R4M	2 x MK 108	
		49 x SG119		
Performance Data				
maximum speed	km/h	1,000	1,000	-
climb speed	km/h	880	675-790	790
ceiling	m	16,000	16,000	0
range at 100 kp thrust				
at 3,000 m altitude	km	64.0	93.5	73.0
at 6,000 m altitude	km	70.0	97.5	74.0
at 9,000 m altitude	km	64.0	92.0	60.6
at 12,000 m altitude	km	55.0	81.0	41.5
Climb angle after takeoff	%	60	60	54
time to climb				
to 3,000 m	s	21	22	33
to 6,000 m	s	36	37	50
to 9,000 m	s	48	52	66
to 12,000 m	s	63	67.5	84
combat time at 100 kp thrust				
at 3,000 m	min	4.6	7.4	5.95
at 6,000 m	min	5.15	7.8	6.1
at 9,000 m	min	4.85	7.45	5.25
at 12,000 m	min	3.9	6.75	3.9
takeoff acceleration	m/s²	21.5	19.5	-
altitude at RATO pod jettison	m	1,180	1,050	-
speed at RATO pod jettison	m/s	221	216	-
time to RATO pod jettison	s	10	10	-

Notes:

1. The HWK 109-559 is often shown as the designation for the engine type used in the Ba 349A and Ba 349B. This was a special derivative of the HWK 109-509 A-2 with the cruise combustion chamber removed, leaving only the main chamber for use. This resulted in a controllable thrust ranging from 150 to 1,700 kp.

2. Documentation with a later date shows the HWK 109-509 D-1 rocket engine planned for the Ba 349B.

92

Ba 349A Technical Layout

Role: vertical takeoff interceptor

Crew: one pilot

Wings: cantilever mid-wing design of wooden construction, rectangular shape with symmetrical profile and 12% chord at 40% chord taper. Constructed of main spar, support spar, five ribs and plywood skinning (2 to 3 mm); the wing end caps incorporate glider shoes for the launch rail; no ailerons or flaps; ailerons incorporated into horizontal stabilizers; 1%angle of attack in relation to the fuselage axis.

Fuselage: comprising the components of forward section, center section and tail cone with empennage; all fuselage components of monocoque construction using 30 x 40 mm laminated wood bulkheads (pine or fir), 20 x 20 mm wooden stringers (pine) and plywood skinning (2-5 mm in nose area, 3 mm in center section, and 2-3 mm in aft section). For production versions, skinning was to have been of 4-5 mm fiberboard, dispensing with the need for the stringers. The skin was comprised of dozens of small sections, with little need for formed skinning.

                      Forward fuselage with plexiglas nose (covering the weapons system) attached to the nose/center section separation point by four bolts; built on a total of five bulkheads.

                      Pilot housed in an enclosed cockpit; 15 mm armor plating ahead of and behind the seat, forward fixed section of the canopy frame made of 2 mm steel plating supporting the side plexiglas plates (10 mm thick) and the front windscreen (60 mm armored glass); entry hatch made of pine/fir bulkheads with stringers and 3 mm plywood skin, with the inner skin made of 2.5 mm plywood.

                      Fuselage center section comprises 9 bulkheads and stringers; supports fuel tanks, pilot's seat (formed plywood sheeting with seatbelt) and wing structure; the all-through wing spar and support spar are bolted onto the bulk heads; entry hatch attached to the fuselage center section using hinges; the center/aft section separation point joined by 20 tension bolts (12 mm I); *T-Stoff* tank above and *C-Stoff* tank below the wings; two recovery parachutes beneath the wing pass-through; rocket engine mounted to the aft separation bulkhead.

                      Fuselage aft section comprises six bulkheads; rocket engine also attached to bulkhead 18.

Control surfaces: cantilever empennage in cruciform shape comprising non-moving tailplane and rudder; tailfins made of wood covered with 3 mm plywood skin; rudder made of tubular steel frame (40 mmI), wooden ribs and 2 mm plywood skin; tailplane joined to the vertical fin at a special attachment point; all four control surfaces fitted with rudders (all with symmetrical profiles); differential elevators for aileron control; rudder control via rods and torsion shafts; jettisonable supplemental panels for the tailplane on takeoff; additional jet flow rudder behind the rocket exhaust; lower vertical fin fitted with steel glider shoe for the launch frame.

Undercarriage: none

Engine: 1 x HWK 109-509 A-2 with 150-1,700 thrust in the aft fuselage and 2 x Schmidding 109-533 (SG34) solid fuel rockets, each with 1,200 kp thrust (four solid fuel rockets for the Ba 349B) located on either side of the aft fuselage; *T-Stoff* tank system holds 365 liters (or 400 liters with the Ba 349B) and the *C-Stoff* tank system holds 165 liters (or 190 liters with the Ba 349B).

Military equipment: 24 unguided Hs 217 *Föhn* rockets or 33 unguided R4M rockets in a battery located in the nose, with simple targeting sight on the forward upper nose area.

DFS

DFS 228

By 1939 the DFS had already experimented with glider flights up to altitudes of 11,600 meters. Based on the results of these flights, as well as the theoretical foundations for stratospheric flights worked out in 1941, it was not difficult to support the idea of a rocket propelled sailplane when the RLM issued a contract for the development of a high altitude reconnaissance aircraft in 1941.

The fundamental concept was completed by February 1942 and was based on a two-step ladder as the aircraft climbed to operating altitude. The first step was to either tow or carry the plane to an altitude of several thousand meters, where its internal engine would be started and then boost the plane to its operating altitude. Its payload for such flights would be cameras weighing about 50 kilograms.

In September 1942 the DFS submitted an initial design description for the high altitude reconnaissance platform. This included the following weight table:

airframe:	885 kg
tank system and engine:	220 kg
empty weight	= 1,105 kg
pilot	100 kg
payload	50 kg
fuel	2,500 kg
takeoff weight	= 3,755 kg

The document listed the following external dimensions:

wingspan	17.40 m
length	10.12 m
height	2.60 m

But from then on work on the program continued quite sporadically and with low priority, which is why in 1943 the RLM issued a priority requirement for the reconnaissance airplane and simultaneously arranged for construction to begin. The official designation was to be the DFS 228. Despite this, it took until early 1944 for overall construction to be finished.

One of the main problems of the DFS was that the high altitude reconnaissance plane would require a pressurized cockpit, but because it was designed as a sailplane this would mean that it could only be built using alloys.

The entire forward fuselage was, as the sole metal component of the airframe, designed as the pressurized area. This was a cylindrical body with a hemispherical forward and aft section. The cockpit was double planked and had thermal insulation (50 mm) made of aluminum foil between the inner and outer skins. In addition, heating cartridges manufactured by IG Farben could also be carried, which generated heat as they broke down and only gave off oxygen. The pilot would fly the aircraft in the prone position in order to present the smallest possible fuselage cross section. Initially the nose section consisted of four panes for pilot visibility, although these were later replaced by a spherical curved plexiglass cover. The pressurized cabin was designed to maintain pressure to altitudes of 8,000 meters, but above that an oxygen mask had to be worn. The entire airframe of the DFS 228 was built of wood, with the fuselage center section housing the skid well, fuel tanks, the rocket engine, and two infrared cameras built by the Zeiss Company. The aft fuselage section held the rocket engine's combustion chamber.

The wings, empennage, fuselage center section, and aft section were completed by May 1944, and final assembly of the DFS 228 V1 began in April 1944 at the DFS in Ainring. Because of delays in the availability of equipment and parts the aircraft was not actually completed until August 1944, and even then without its rocket engine, for the originally planned BMW 3390A rocket propulsion system continued to exhibit problems with its fuel feed. Additionally, it had

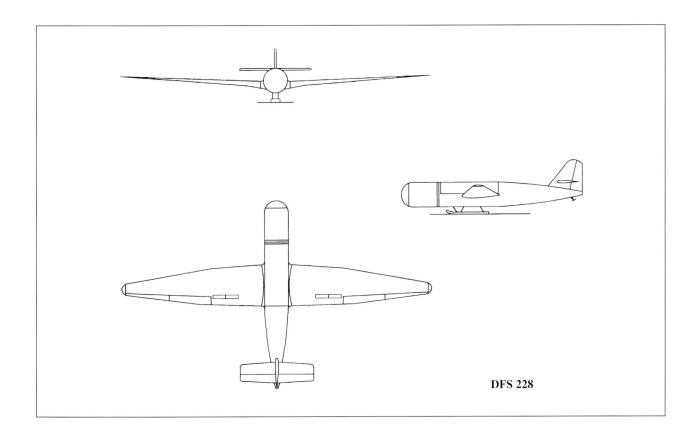

DFS 228

been recently discovered that the four glass panels offered the pilot inadequate visibility, which meant that the V1's nose required modification yet again. The DFS 228 V1 was, therefore, initially evaluated as a glider. It was accordingly given the registration D-IBFQ.

In early 1945 the V2 was also finally available for flight testing. Unlike the V1, the V2 was already kitted out with a rocket motor, dive brakes, and cameras. The selected engine was the HWK 109-509 A-1, which was also used in the Me 163 B, since the BMW rocket engine never made it into production.

With the final months of the war as a backdrop the RLM only contracted for the assembly of 10 prototypes, which were to be issued to field units in 1945. There were no further plans for any larger production orders.

The DFS 228's method of operation was established as follows:

1. Carried to an altitude of 10,000 meters on the back of a specially modified Do 217 K-3.
2. The two aircraft separate, and then a climb under rocket power to an altitude of 22,500 meters.
3. Holding this altitude for 45 minutes by sporadic bursts of the rocket motor and completion of its photoreconnaissance mission.
4. Return by gliding down to an altitude of 12,000 meters, which meant that a distance of 750 km could be covered
5. From an altitude of 12,000 meters a distance of 315 km could be traversed, but at these altitudes enemy fighters had to be reckoned with. Therefore, the remaining fuel was to have been used for maneuvering out of harm's way at this level.

DFS 228 V2 Technical Data:	
wingspan	17.55 m
length	10.50 m
empty weight	1,350 kg
takeoff weight	4,210 kg
maximum speed	900 km/h

DFS 228 on its test mother plane, a Dornier Do 217M. (Dornier archives)

	DFS 228 Type Description:
Role:	high altitude rocket powered reconnaissance plane
Crew:	one pilot lying prone in a pressurized cockpit comprising the fuselage nose section
Wings:	cantilever midwing design, double tapered with slight sweepback. Wooden construction. Main spar running wingtip to wingtip, wing halves made of wooden ribs and completely covered with plywood skin. Two section ailerons made of wood with fabric covering, with the inner section functioning as flaps during landing. Spoilers on the wing upper and lower surfaces. Angle of attack in relation to fuselage axis is 4.5%.
Fuselage:	three section fuselage with circular cross section. Forward section comprises a pressurized cockpit made of metal; center and aft sections are of wooden monocoque construction. Fuselage center section includes wing attachments and fuel tank mounts. Separation bulkhead between the fuselage center and aft sections also serves as engine mount.
Control surfaces:	cantilever standard empennage made of wood, single spar fins covered in plywood, rudder in fabric. Horizontal stabilizers mounted high on vertical stabilizer with adjustable angle of attack. Two part horizontal stabilizer with simple counterbalanced elevators. Vertical rudder also counterbalanced with additional powered servo tabs (Flettner servo tabs).
Undercarriage:	wide, retractable metal skid beneath the fuselage center section and tailskid
Engine:	1 x Walter HWK 109-509 A-1 liquid fuel rocket engine offering 1,600 kp static thrust, which can be throttled back to 100 kp. Tanks for the *C-* and *T-Stoff* fuels located in fuselage center section.
Military equipment:	no armament, two Zeiss infra-red aerial photography cameras

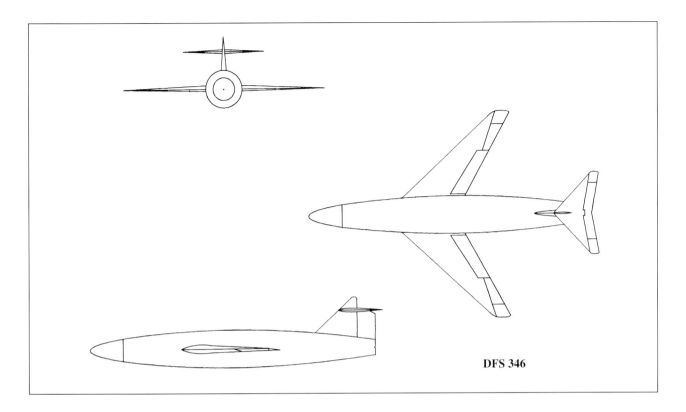

DFS 346

At that time, the standard bailout procedure would not save the life of a pilot at such high altitudes. Here, too, new paths had to be charted:

1. The entire pressurized cockpit could separate from the main fuselage by four explosive bolts. These could be set off with a lever by the pilot.
2. Stabilized by a small parachute, the cockpit, together with the nose, would fall to an altitude of about 4,000 meters.
3. Controlled by a barometer, at this altitude the plexiglass screen would automatically drop away and the pilot on his bed would slide out forward.
4. At a certain safety distance from the cockpit the bed automatically dropped away from the pilot and his parachute would then deploy.

Before the war's end the two prototypes underwent intensive testing, including at the Rechlin test center, giving satisfactory results.

When the American troops reached Ainring in May 1945 they found, only slightly damaged, the DFS 228 V1 fitted with a Walter rocket motor. The odd looking plane was shipped to the RAE at Farnborough *in toto* and there examined. It then lost its skid, and was probably immediately scrapped without further ado.

Allied troops supposedly also found the DFS 228 V2 at Hörsching, near Linz, although its subsequent whereabouts are unknown.

DFS 346

In the years 1943 and 1944 a phenomenon kept appearing with the new jets then in development, such as the Me 262 and the Ar 234. At higher speeds the theoretical calculations with regard to aerodynamics, flight mechanics, and flight performance did not agree with wind tunnel research, and bore only the slightest resemblance to test flight results. To be sure, it had been recognized that by sweeping the wing, it was possible to delay the onset of compressibility (boundary layer) in the transonic region to higher speeds; nevertheless, the actual results lagged behind the calculated predictions. It was thus imperative that the necessary scientific knowledge be acquired relative to engine performance at high altitudes, as well as flight mechanics and aerodynamics at higher speeds. It should be noted that around this time the RLM had recognized (was forced to recognize) that, compared to piston powered fighters, the jet airplane was the markedly superior choice, if not the only one, to counter the enemy's bombing raids.

The RLM therefore, in the summer of 1944, issued a contract to the DFS for the development of a single-seat experimental design able to operate at high altitudes and high supersonic speeds. The design's starting point was to be the DFS 228. The project was designated the DFS 346. It was planned to make use of two Walter liquid fuel rocket engines. The primary goal was to investigate whether existing technology might be able to penetrate the sound barrier, and what type of aeromechanical problems could be expected just prior to and during penetration of the barrier.

Because of the anticipated high fuel consumption rate during the climb phase, the DFS 346—like its DFS 228 predecessor—would be carried piggy-back to an altitude of 10,000 meters, where it would climb to over 20,000 meters under its own power and reach a speed of 2,270 km/h (greater than Mach 2.0!).

Work began in August 1944, initially with experiments using a tapered wing having a sweep of 45 degrees, at the *Institut für Aerodynamik und Flugmechanik*.

Many details of the DFS 228 were borrowed for the design work on the DFS 346, e.g. the prone pilot configuration on a bed with chin support in a pressurized cabin. One unique feature, however, was the arrangement of the instruments so that they did not obstruct the pilot's view. Some of the instruments could be read using mirrors, without the pilot having to move his head. The rescue system used in the DFS 228 was also used again. New for the DFS 346, however, was the fact that the forward section of the pressurized cockpit was made of a hemispherical plexiglass cover that, for aerodynamic reasons, fit into another cover that blended directly into the fuselage profile. Warm air to prevent icing was blown into the space between the two covers. In addition, the DFS 346 was fitted with a nose pitot tube. Because of the requirement for supersonic flight the DFS 346 had to be fitted with swept wings and was made entirely of metal.

By the end of November 1944 the design work had been completed, including the design description being drawn up. The Siebel Flugzeugwerke in Halle, on the Saale, was contracted for the completion of the DFS 346, since the DFS had no experience whatsoever with metal aircraft construction. The DFS, however, was to carry out associated wind tunnel testing.

When the American troops reached Halle in April 1945 they found at the Siebel Works several prototypes in advanced stages of construction. Even though the DFS 346 never appeared in America, there were indications that the Americans—as part of the agreed upon evacuation of the area in June 1945—took with them a "prototype of a new supersonic aircraft" and 23 former Siebel employees.

Once the Soviet forces assumed control of Halle, work continued at Siebel under its new Soviet owners. Along with other companies in the Soviet zone of occupation, Siebel too received the status of a "special design bureau" (Siebel: OKB 3). From that time onward the aircraft was known as the Siebel 346 (Si 346). The primary interest, in addition to the aerodynamics, was mainly focused on the Walter rocket engine.

From 22 October 1946 onward all special design bureaus in the zone of occupation were dissolved and relocated into Soviet territory. The former OKB 3 at the Siebel Company was moved into Experimental Works I at Podberes'ye, about 120 km north of Moscow, and with it about 20% of about 700 Siebel workers and their families. Within this complex was housed

DFS 346 Type Description:	
Role:	supersonic experimental aircraft
Crew:	one pilot lying prone in a pressurized cockpit comprising the fuselage nose section
Wings:	all-metal cantilever two section design with a 45% sweepback. Control surfaces running the entire trailing edge, with ailerons in the middle and hydraulic flaps on the inner wing sections as well as small high speed ailerons also used for trimming on the outer wings.
Fuselage:	all-metal cantilever fuselage with circular cross section in three parts. Forward section designed as a pressurized cockpit with glazed nose. Center section houses the fuel tanks and the skid. Aft section supports the engine and empennage.
Control surfaces:	cantilever all-metal standard empennage. All surfaces designed with a 45% sweepback. Horizontal stabilizers in T-form mounted on vertical stabilizer
Undercarriage:	wide, retractable metal skid.
Engine:	2 x Walter HWK 109-509 B-1 liquid fuel rocket engines each offering 2,000 kp static thrust. Three tanks for the *C*- and *T-Stoff* fuels located in fuselage center section.
Military equipment:	no armament, two Zeiss infra-red aerial photography cameras

an OKB 1 (Junkers) and an OKB 2, in which primarily Siebel people worked. In addition, an Si 346 built in Halle was sent to the Soviet Union.

In Experimental Works I the problem of premature separation of the boundary layer from the wings was solved. Following comprehensive wind tunnel tests, the upper surfaces of the wings were fitted with boundary layer fences.

However, additional testing was hindered by an initial lack of suitable carrier planes, plus there were problems with the availability of the special rocket fuels (*C-Stoff* and *T-Stoff*) and the absence of critical materials and equipment. Not to mention the language barrier, and the fact that all documents needed to be matched to Soviet blueprint standards.

Flight testing began in 1948 with glider trials at the Toplistan airfield (8 km from the Moscow city limits). A suitable carrier plane was finally found in 1949. It was one of three Boeing B-29s from the U.S. Army Air Force that had made an emergency landing in the territory of the Soviet Union and now served as a pattern for the design of the Tupolev Tu-4 strategic bomber. After 1949 a Tu-4 was used for test flights. All experimental flights were made by the German test pilot Wolfgang Ziese, since there was no suitable Russian pilot able to fly the Si 346. Pilot Ziese had been trained for this on *Kranich* and *Grunau IIB* sailplanes modified in-house by fitting them with a reclining cockpit.

In June 1950 the Si 346 V3 was completed using Soviet-built Walter rocket engines. Initial flights were conducted with the engine switched off. Test flights under its own power began in August 1951 and ended with the crash of the Si 346 V3 on 14 September 1951, due to a wing fracture at an altitude of 20,000 meters. Thanks to the rescue system, Wolfgang Ziese was able to survive by blowing off the pressurized cockpit once the airframe reached lower altitudes. After that the program was officially ended, not least because since 1947 there were those in the Soviet aviation ministry who held the view that the German scientists and engineers were scientifically "burned out" and should be sent back home. Otherwise, in order to gain any further use from these people they would need to be brought up to current Soviet developments. This, however, was not desired.

Test results of the Si 346 flight test program have not been published by Russia to date. Therefore, it cannot be stated with any degree of certainty whether or not the German engineers and Wolfgang Ziese succeeded in breaking the sound barrier with the Si 346. Based on its layout, though, the airplane was entirely capable of doing so.

Focke-Wulf

Focke-Wulf Project VI *Flitzer*

During the years 1943/44 Focke-Wulf worked on various jet powered projects as alternatives to the Messerschmitt Me 262. These were numbered in chronological order with Roman numerals.

In March 1943 the first design (Project I) was completed, envisioning a turbojet engine beneath the forward fuselage and with a tailwheel. The Project II design from June 1943 was virtually identical to the previous design, with the exception of the nosewheel now included. The third design (Project III) was to have had the turbojet engine integrated into the fuselage, with the addition of a dual rudder. The design of Project IV from December 1943 was generally the same as that of Project III, but had twin booms. Project V from January 1944 was ultimately developed as the *Huckebein* jet fighter.

Developmental work on the *Huckebein* project, however, raised so many questions that Focke-Wulf decided to develop a simpler structured jet fighter parallel to it. The starting point would be the Project IV, which was to be further developed as Project VI. Main features were the integration of a Heinkel He S011 turbojet engine in the aft fuselage and the installation of a rocket engine beneath the fuselage. The twin booms supporting the empennage would be carried over from Project IV for Project VI.

On 1 February 1944 an initial design description (no. 272) was completed for Project VI. According to it, the main criteria in the layout were:

- use of a rocket motor to supplement the jet engine for the purpose of attaining high climb rates
- heavy armament, consisting of 2 x MK 108 cannons and 2 x MG 151 machine guns
- pressurized cockpit
- 830 km/h maximum speed

The use of a rocket engine for achieving a high climb rate leads us to believe that Focke-Wulf most likely intended the Project VI to be a fast climbing interceptor rather than a standard pursuit fighter.

The rocket motor was to have been provided by HWK (type 109-509B). Required thrust was specified at 1,900 kp. The system was to have been delivered completely assembled and functional, only requiring its installation beneath the jet engine in the airplane's tail section.

The rocket system was to have comprised the following elements:

- pump system (turbine with *C-* and *T-Stoff* pumps)
- primer tank for the *C-Stoff*
- steam generator
- stop valves (between the steam generator and the primer tank)
- pressure regulator
- governor/throttle
- filter for the *C-Stoff*
- combustion chamber
- drain vent

Under an agreement with the test center at Karlshagen the fuel tanks for the *T-Stoff* were to have been manufactured from a copper-free alloy, particularly aluminum, whereas the *C-Stoff* tanks would be made of the standard fuel tank materials. For the *T-Stoff* lines, seals, and sleeves the plastic mipolam would be used, and buna plastic for the *C-Stoff* lines, seals, and sleeves.

Detailed trim computations were completed for type description no. 272 by 20 March 1944, and one day later, on 21 March, the weight balance for Project VI (based on type description no. 272) had been drawn up.

One of the most telling features of the *Flitzer* at this early stage was the split air intake for the jet engine. The air intakes were located in the wing roots on either side of the fuselage, a design feature that caused a loss in thrust for the jet engine of 6.5 to 7%.

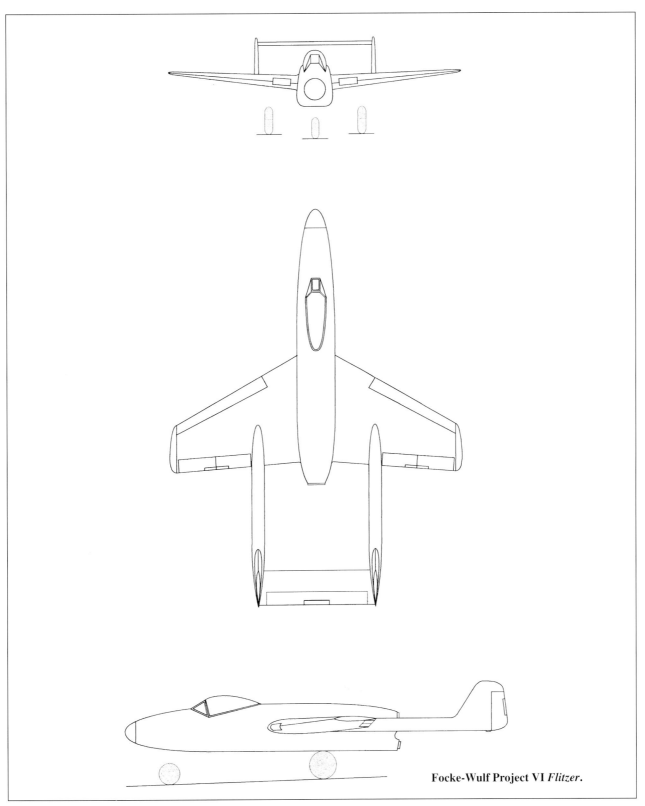

Focke-Wulf Project VI *Flitzer*.

In June 1944 Focke-Wulf began working on the design of the *Flitzer*. Initially, there were serious problems with the installation of the wing armament (MG 151/20), because these were to have been located quite close to the main gear—ultimately causing structural and stability problems.

Over the course of project design the *Flitzer* underwent various stages of development, in which the dimensioning of the wings with regard to chord and aspect ratio was tweaked repeatedly to reflect the various takeoff weights. On the other hand, the fuselage remained unchanged.

101

Fw *Flitzer* Design Layout

Role: interceptor

Crew: one pilot

Wings: tapered outline with 23% sweep along a 25% line, symmetrical profile with 40% tapered chord and a constant trailing edge sweep of 15%, with two ailerons on each outer wing. The inner aileron can be used as a landing flap. Movement of the outer aileron is Å20%; movement of the inner aileron is Å5%, or + 30% when functioning as a landing flap. Ailerons built of wood. Also located on the inner wing area (between fuselage and tailboom) is a hydraulically activated single unit split flap for landing with a maximum deviation of 75%.

Fuselage: The fuselage consists of the following components: nose cap, forward section, aft section (including engine support) and tailbooms. The nose cap is made of wood. The forward fuselage section includes the cockpit (pressurized), the weapons bay (including ammunition), the nose gear, the radio equipment and two fuel tanks. The fuselage aft section is connected to the middle section by means of bolts. The aft section houses the two propulsion units, with the turbojet engine above and the rocket engine below a dividing panel. The two identical tailbooms are affixed to the wings (1.60 m either side of the fuselage centerline) using bolt flanges. The tailbooms, made of alloy, have a cylindrical cross section (I 336 mm) and a length of 2.15 m. They function as a tank for the rocket fuel (content 156 liters) and are therefore seal riveted.

Control surfaces: Control surfaces are divided into wing control surfaces (ailerons and landing flaps) and the tail surfaces (vertical and horizontal stabilizers). The horizontal stabilizer is located between the two tailbooms, has a surface area of 2.87 m², and a span of 3.20 m. The tailplane is a two spar design and can be electrically adjusted in flight from + 2% to -3%. The single piece elevator is made of duraluminum ribs covered in fabric and is aerodynamically and weight counterbalanced. The maximum deviation for the elevator is -30% to +20%; the trim tab has a movement of is -10% to +15%.

The dual vertical stabilizers have a surface area of 2 x 1.0 m². The tailfin is a two spar design with fixed skinning; the rudder is made of fabric covered duraluminum and has a movement of Å20%.

Undercarriage: hydraulically retractable standard gear. The nose wheel (dimensions of 560 x 200 mm) retracts forward into the fuselage, and the two main wheels (with dimensions of 740 x 210 mm) retract into the wings.

Engine: 1 x HwS 109-011 turbojet engine and 1 x Walter HWK 109-509. The turbojet engine is fitted into the aft fuselage and is fed by two air intakes (located port an starboard in the wing roots). The rocket system is located beneath the turbojet (separated by a firewall panel) and is aligned so that the powerline of the thrust vector runs through the aircraft center of gravity.

The tank system comprises a fuselage group (470 liters and 200 liters), a wing tank group in the outer wing sections (each 300 liters) and a tank group in the tailbooms (each 156 liters).

Military equipment: 2 x MK 108 in the fuselage with an optional 2 x MG 151/20 in the wings. The compressed air canisters for reloading the MK 108s are located between the two cannons on the floor.
Plans call for the use of the Revi 16c sight.
Armor protection against 12.7 mm ammunition both fore and aft
FuG 15Y and FuG 25a
fire extinguisher system

On 5 July 1944 type description no. 280 for a single engine jet fighter with rocket engine was published, with the layout of the Fw *Flitzer* now corresponding directly to the information given in the table on page 102.

Up to this time all installation blueprints were drawn up for the V6 prototype of the Heinkel He S 011 jet engine. This prototype belonged to the first batch of prototype engines (V1 through V25) of the He S 011, all of which differed from each other in one aspect or another. During the summer of 1944 the Hirth Works began production of the second lot of prototype engines. This second batch included engines V26 through V85, all of which were identical to each other and to be used for the type certification of the engine. Delivery of these 60 jet engines was to take place between September 1944 and January 1945. At total of five of these new powerplants were reserved for the *Flitzer* project. Taking the delivery timetable for this engine into account, it was estimated that the *Flitzer's* first prototype with the He S 011 engine would be cleared for flight on 15 March 1945.

It was eventually discovered that the production version of the He S 011 would take up more room in the airplane's fuselage than originally anticipated, meaning that the fuselage required modification in both its cross sectiona and its length.

For its part, the RLM showed no interest whatsoever in the Focke-Wulf design; on the contrary, on 10 September 1944 at Oberammergau the RLM announced that, after reviewing all the jet fighter designs submitted, there was simply no alternative to the Me 262. As a result, Focke-Wulf submitted a "rougher" design of the *Flitzer* that would not only be easier to produce, but also be powered by the BMW 003A jet engine in place of the originally intended He S011. The Heinkel engine would only be used in later models, after it had reached its production maturity. Yet this new proposal also fell on deaf ears within the RLM. When, by November 1944 the He S 011 still was not ready to go into production, the RLM canceled the *Flitzer* project altogether.

Within Focke-Wulf itself, though, the plans were officially carried on the list of jet fighter projects up until 11 December 1944, when they were replaced by those of the Ta 183 *Huckebein*. Focke-Wulf managed to complete a mockup of the *Flitzer* by the time the program was canceled.

On a final note, it is worth mentioning that, with the exception of the supplemental rocket engine, the layout of the Focke-Wulf *Flitzer* is virtually identical to that of the de Havilland Vampire produced in England after the war.

Design Drafts on the Basis of the *Flitzer*						
		Flitzer	*Flitzer*	*Volksflitzer*	*Flitzer*	*Flitzer*
Date		2/1/1944	7/5/1944	9/15/1944	9/18/1944	10/3/1944
Length	m	10.55	10.55	10.55	10.55	10.55
Height	m	2.35	2.35	2.35	2.35	2.35
Span	m	8.00	8.00	8.00	8.00	8.00
Wing area	m²	15.50	17.00	14.00	17.00	14.00
Takeoff weight	kg	4,750	4,820	3,150	3,660	3,650
Fuel	kg	1,170	1,230	660	830	830
Engine		109-011	109-011	109-003	109-011	109-011
	109-509	109-509				
Max. speed						
at sea level	km/h	785	805	700	810	860
at 3000 m altitude	km/h	815	865	740	855	925
at 6000 m altitude	km/h	830	908	770	915	965
at 9000 m altitude	km/h	825	925	740	935	975
at 12000 m altitude	km/h	800	913		910	950
time to climb to 9000 m	min	12.0		23.0		9.4
Service ceiling	m	13,000	13,800	10,700	13,800	14,100
Range						
at 3000 m altitude	km	680		350		500
at 6000 m altitude	km	890		1,100	600	660
Armament		2 x MK 108 (60 rounds plus 2 x MG 151 at 175 rounds)	2 x MK 108 (80 rounds)	2 x MK 108 (60 rounds)	2 x MK 108 (80 rounds)	2 x MK 108 (60 rounds)

Arado

Arado Ar 234 R

As early as the end of 1940 the RLM issued a request for tender for the development of a jet powered long-range reconnaissance aircraft with a range of 2,200 km as a replacement for the Ju 88 P. The victor in the bidding battle was the Arado company with its E 370 proposal, which was subsequently developed into the Ar 234. Design work was underway by early 1941 but, as a result of the serious problems that BMW and Junkers continued to have with the development of the jet engine, the first flight of the Ar 234 V1 did not occur until 14 June 1943 at the Rheine airbase. The first V1 through V8 prototypes all had a centerline landing skid and two support skids, a configuration which was later found to have serious disadvantages. Just one of the reasons why the projected A-series was scrapped.

Arado Ar 234 V9 made its first flight on 12 March 1944. This was the first prototype of the B-series. The most significant difference between the B-series and the originally planned A-series was the incorporation of a wheeled undercarriage to replace the centerline skid and the two support skids. The B-series was initially conceived of as a reconnaissance type and developed into the B-0 (13 aircraft for testing at Rechlin) and the B01 series. Shortly after production of the B-1 began, though, the program switched to the B-2 high speed bomber series.

Just four days after the V9's maiden flight Arado submitted a concept study for an Ar 234 R high speed rocket powered reconnaissance plane, based on the B-series. This high speed design was intended for short range and altitudes of 17,000 meters. At this operating altitude the aircraft would be well out of reach of enemy fighters, whose ceiling at this time was around 12,500 meters. There were two different avenues explored with regard to the aircraft's rocket propulsion:

1. Installation of a rocket motor beneath each wing (on the attachment points of the jet engines). These rocket engines would offer an acceleration thrust

of 1,500 kp each and a cruise thrust of 400 kp. The takeoff weight of the aircraft in this configuration was 9,100 kg.

2. Installation of a single HWK 109-509 rocket motor beneath the airplane's tail. This system would offer a total thrust of 2,400 kp and a cruise thrust of 400 kp. To this end, the rocket engine contained two separate combustion chambers: a main combustor, that would only be used for climbing thrust and would deliver 2,000 kp; and a cruise chamber that would generate 400 kp thrust. The feeder lines for the engine would run outside along the aircraft's skin and be covered, so that there would be little actual modification to the design compared to the B-series.

By 22 March 1944 the first blueprints for the Ar 234 R had been completed. These already showed that, with a nod to the high operating altitudes at 17,000 meters, there were plans to make use of a pressurized cockpit. Although B-series prototypes (V9 through V12) sometimes used pressurized cockpits, the subsequent B-0, B-1, and B-2 series were produced without pressurization. For this reason the pressurized cockpit of the C-series, just entering development at the time, had to be used.

Another important requirement of the military was that the Ar 234 R's flight performance had to be better than that of the P-51 Mustang and P-47 Thunderbolt high performance fighters. The RLM had been aware of the performance data for these aircraft types since April 1944.

On 24 May 1944 the first theoretical performance calculations for the Ar 234 R were submitted, which took into account the second propulsion alternative using the HWK 109-509 rocket system. In addition, it was assumed that in order to give the aircraft any type of useful range it would have to be towed to an altitude of about 8,000 meters. The aircraft proposed to do the job was the He 177, with its DB 610 engines,

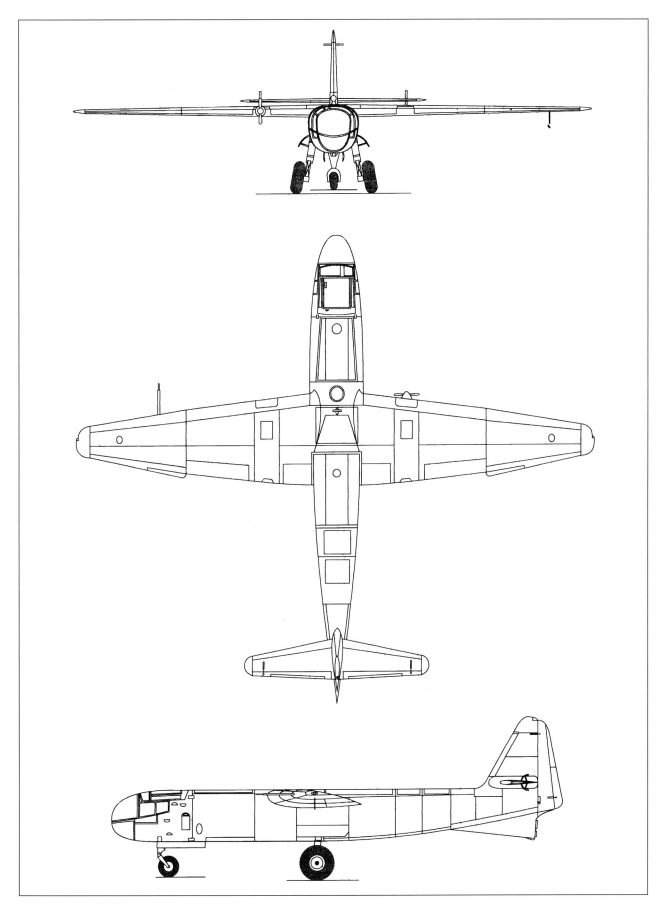

Arado Ar 234R

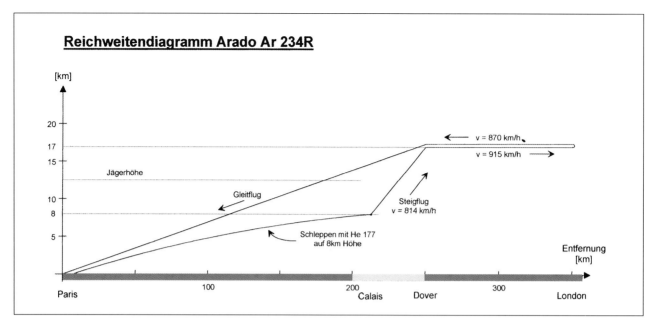

Reichweitendiagramm Arado Ar 234R

[km]

20
17
15

Jägerhöhe

Gleitflug

10
8

Steigflug
v = 814 km/h

5

Schleppen mit He 177
auf 8km Höhe

v = 870 km/h
v = 915 km/h

Entfernung
[km]

Paris
100
200
Calais
Dover
300
London

Range diagram and mission profile for the Ar 234R.

since the wing loading of both airplanes was almost identical. A requirement for a loiter time of 2 hours and 20 minutes was established, which consisted of the following profile:

- towed takeoff from its operating base in the vicinity of Paris
- towed climb to Calais, where it would be released
- climb under its own power to 17,000 meters (achieved somewhere over Dover)
- flight to the target area at a speed of 915 km/h
- return from the operating area at a speed of 870 km/h
- initiation of descent back to Paris over the English Channel

The RLM ordered work on this project halted on 3 June 1944. The role of the Ar 234 R was to be taken over by the four-engined C-series, whose development had advanced considerably in the meantime and whose first prototype, the Ar 234 V19, flew on its maiden flight on 30 September 1944.

Parallel to this project of a short range, high altitude recon plane, Arado explored the operational potential of the Ar 234 as a pursuit fighter. The basis for this was to be the four-jet Ar 234C, powered by four BMW 003A turbojet engines. These powerplants offered 800 kp of static thrust each. A pursuit fighter must possess good enough climb performance to be able to intercept enemy aircraft when they are already in view, or on the return leg. Therefore, it was proposed to replace two of the BMW 003A jet engines with two BMW 003R engines. These BMW 003R consisted of a BMW 003A turbojet engine onto which was mated a BMW 109-718 rocket engine with 1,250 kp of thrust. This was the same engine that had also been envisioned for the Me 262 C-2b Interceptor II project. The additional *T-Stoff* fuel needed for the rocket system was to have been carried in 600 liter drop tanks carried under each engine nacelle.

The testbed for this configuration was the Ar 234 V16 (*Werknr.* 130 026, registration markings PH+SW), with two BMW 003R engines, which was to have been used for high speed trials. To this end four different wings were produced for the V16:

- one swept wing made of wood with outward swept outer sections (called a "crescent wing" today)
- one straight wing
- two swept wings with laminar profile

106

The V16 was never tested, as the BMW 003R engine did not reach production maturity by the time the war ended, nor was any prototype engine ever sent to the Arado Company. This airplane's final resting place remains unknown to this day.

In spite of all this, Arado issued a report dated 27 January 1945 on the theoretical flight performance figures of the Ar 234C with two BMW 003A and two BMW 003R engines. The report included the following calculated performance data:

- maximum speed: 900 km/h at 11,000 meters' altitude
- theoretical maximum speed: 960 km/h
- maximum climb speed: 60 m/s (including the two rocket engines, each with 1,250 kp thrust)
- maximum service ceiling: 15,000 meters
- maximum endurance: 1 hr 12 min

Because of the problems with the BMW 003R engines and the sharp restrictions brought about by the war in its last few months, the Ar 234C project as a pursuit fighter never came to fruition.

Using the Ar 234B configuration as a basis, the layout of the Ar 234 R was as follows:

Role: short range high altitude reconnaissance plane

Crew: one pilot

Wings: cantilever all metal shoulderwing design, double tapered with slight sweepback. Single piece, two spar tapered wings. Hydraulically powered split landing flaps. With flaps set, ailerons are dropped by 10%

Fuselage: all metal monocoque fuselage, ejection seat, pressurized cockpit and braking parachute

Control surfaces: cantilever standard empennage with mechanically adjustable tailplane and rudder trim, with partial elevator/rudder counterbalance

Undercarriage: retractable tricycle undercarriage on single unit shock absorbing struts, nose gear retracting aft into the fuselage nose and main gear retracting into either side of the fuselage.

Engine: 1 x Walter HWK 109-509C liquid fuel rocket engine offering 2,400 kp total thrust and 400 kp cruise thrust located beneath the tail. 3,500 kg fuel capacity carried internally in the fuselage

Military equipment: 2 x Rb 50/30 or
2 x Rb 75/30 or
1 x Rb 75/30 and 1 x Rb 20/30

The following weight and thrust data were projected for this short range high altitude reconnaissance version:

empty equipped weight	3,500 kg
fuel	3,500 kg
crew	100 kg
takeoff weight	= 7,100 kg
climb thrust	2,000 + 400 kp = 2,400 kp
cruise thrust	400 kp
wing loading	263 - 133.5 kg/m^2
thrust/weight ratio	0.338 kp/kg

Gothaer Waggonfabrik

Go 345 Precision Landing Aircraft

One of the most adventuresome designs for a rocket powered aircraft coming out of Germany's aviation industry has to be the Go 345 in its version as a precision landing plane. Starting in early 1944 the Gothaer Waggonfabrik began working on its Project P-53Z, a successor to its reliable Go 242/244 transport glider models.

A key design criterion for this project was the ability to make a vertical point landing, with the landing area being no greater than the dimensions of the aircraft itself. The intention here was to offer better protection against enemy anti-aircraft defenses, which had a maximum angle of +80% with their barrels. The Gothaer Waggonfabrik even went so far as to assume that the special features required for this precision landing would be independent of the aircraft type. This airplane was to have followed the following operational profile:

- approach to target area under tow or, alternatively, under its own power. In the latter case the airplane was equipped with an Argus-Schmidt ramjet under each wing, which would have enabled a speed of 300 km/h. The use of these ramjets obviated the need for tow planes (which were always in short supply in large scale operations) and their inevitable link to large airfields.
- jettisoning the ramjets upon entry into the target area, to avoid explosions on landing
- initiation of a vertical dive as soon as the airplane is over the landing site, with dive brakes limiting the speed to 300 km/h
- deployment of braking parachute at an altitude of 600 meters, reducing the dive speed to 90 km/h (25 m/s!)
- automatic ignition of the deceleration rockets at 10 meters' altitude, giving a braking effect of about 3.2g
- aircraft reaches the ground at a speed of nearly

0 km/h, with the permissible tolerance ranging between 0 to 5 m/s; a special ring-shaped shock absorber in the nose would be included to cushion impact even further.
- the exhaust from the rockets is so directed as to give a slight rotation along the roll axis, which causes the airplane to tip over to the horizontal after touching down and, based on the rocking horse principle, roll onto a landing skid

In the event of a catastrophe involving failure of the braking rockets, the entire nose would be designed to be collapsible. With a maximum collapsible travel of 1.80 meters this would completely absorb the impact shock that (according to calculations by the Gothaer Waggonfabrik) the crew would be subjected to an acceleration of about 20g for a period of 0.12 seconds. Because of the brief time span and a special seating configuration, the industry's view was that this high g value would pose no danger for the crew.

The automatic firing of the decelerator rockets would have been accomplished by two 10 meter long cables, tensioned with lead weights. Together with the braking 'chute the two lead weights would deploy at an altitude of 600 meters. The two weights were supposed to keep the two cables under constant tension. The cables were connected to an electric switch at their other end, which kept the rockets from firing as long as there was tension on the cables. When the lead weights came in contact with the ground, the tension on the cables would relax and the rockets would immediately fire. Standard solid fuel rockets were envisioned for the braking rockets, which would be housed in the nose.

The aviation industry believed it was able to guarantee the safety of the precision landing concept firstly by only making use of proven components for the dive brakes, braking parachute, and the braking rockets, and secondly, by anticipating and studying potential pitfalls and working out the remedies beforehand. In the

Punktlandung normal

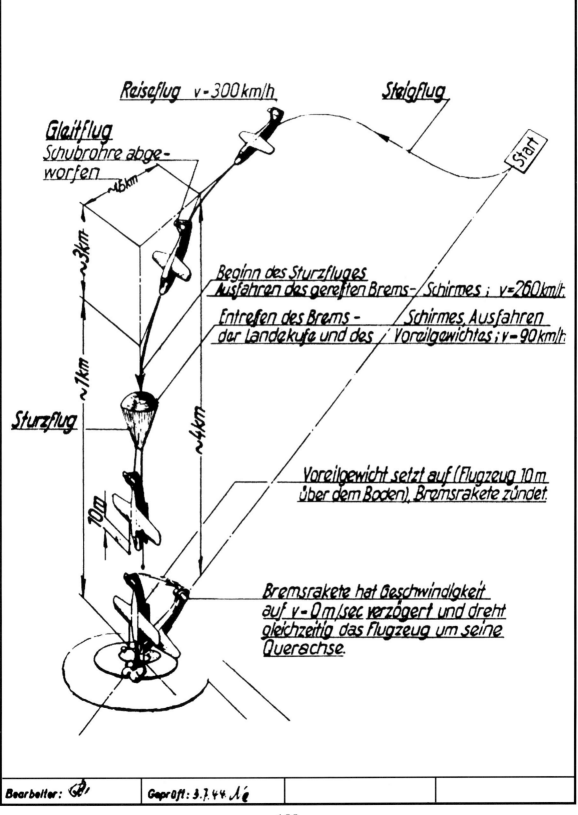

Reiseflug v~300 km/h

Steigflug

Gleitflug

Schubrohre abgeworfen

~6 km

~3 km

~1 km

Start

Sturzflug

Beginn des Sturzfluges
Ausfahren des gerefften Brems-/Schirmes ; v=260 km/h.

Entrefen des Brems - / Schirmes, Ausfahren
der Landekufe und des / Voreilgewichtes ; v~90 km/h.

~4 km

Voreilgewicht setzt auf (Flugzeug 10 m
über dem Boden), Bremsrakete zündet.

10 m

Bremsrakete hat Geschwindigkeit
auf v~0 m/sec verzögert und dreht
gleichzeitig das Flugzeug um seine
Querachse.

Bearbeiter:

Geprüft: 3.7.44

109

Punktlandung Katastrophe

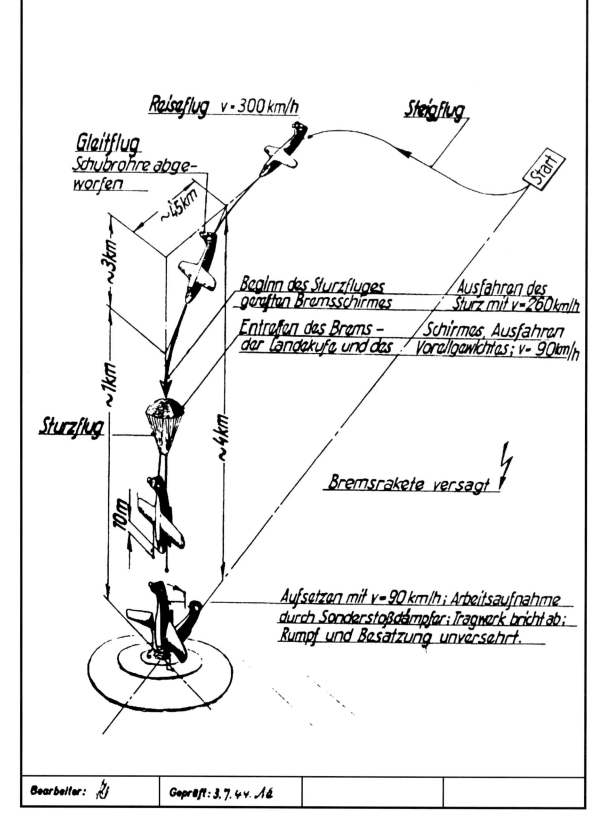

Steigflug

Start

Reiseflug v = 300 km/h

Gleitflug
Schubrohre abge-
worfen

~4,5km

~3km

Beginn des Sturzfluges
gerafften Bremsschirmes

Ausfahren des
Sturz mit v = 260 km/h

Entrefen des Brems –
der Landekufe und des

Schirmes, Ausfahren
Vorallgewichtes; v = 90 km/h

~1km

Sturzflug

~4km

Bremsrakete versagt

70m

Aufsetzen mit v = 90 km/h; Arbeitsaufnahme
durch Sonderstoßdämpfer; Tragwerk bricht ab;
Rumpf und Besatzung unversehrt.

Bearbeiter: Ki   Geprüft: 3.7.44. Ab

110

industry's opinion, there were just two potential pitfalls with regard to the precision landing idea. The first involved the failure of the braking 'chute to deploy. Since this was to happen at an altitude of 600 meters, the pilot was still capable of pulling the airplane out of the dive and making a normal landing. The second danger was a failure of the braking rockets, which in turn might be caused by two things: either the lead weights failed to deploy, or the rocket ignition system was defective. The lead weights also deployed at an altitude of 600 meters, in which event a normal landing was again possible. More critical was a failure of the ignition, as the crew would not notice this until

reaching an altitude of 10 meters—just 0.4 seconds before impact. This scenario, however, would be offset by the catastrophic landing failsafe (collapsible nose).

Looking at this idea from today's perspective, such an operation would seem to be tantamount to a one-way trip to heaven, not to mention the absolute faith in God the crew would need to be able to use such technology.

A layout as an engine-less transport glider was also drawn up in addition to this specialized precision landing airplane. Neither design advanced beyond the project stages and a handful of model tests in the wind tunnel of the DVL in Berlin.

Sänger

Strato-Gleiter

From 1932 onward, as an assistant at the TH Vienna Eugen Sänger was involved in the scientific research of liquid fueled rockets. In this context he carried out no less than 235 experiments within the space of three years, experiments that resulted in a string of patent applications. Among these, for example, was a patent for a high pressure rocket motor with a compression chamber pressure of 60 *bar* and a patent for the principle—still in use today—of regenerative cooling of the combustion chamber using the rocket's fuel.

In 1933 Eugen Sänger published his first book on rocket flight technology, something that resulted in him being called as the director of the German Experimental Rocket Flight Institution, a part of the DVL. This institute was disguised under the title of the Trauen Aviation Test Center and was located near Trauen, on the Lüneburger Heide.

There Eugen Sanger was able to fully dedicate himself to his work. By 1938 the theoretical foundations for a supersonic glider had been worked out, and a model was built to a scale of 1:20. In 1939 Sänger began working on a liquid fuel rocket engine offering 1,000 kp of thrust. This served as the primer for developing an engine actually needed for delivering 100,000 kp of thrust. This enormous demand of thrust was the result of theoretical ideas developed in 1933 and 1938. But the outbreak of the Second World War jeopardized any further work. The only alternative left to Sänger was to pursue his space glider project under military auspices and redesign it as a long-range bomber. This bomber, which Sänger christened

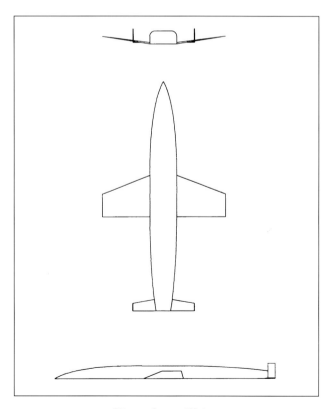

Sänger *Strato-Gleiter*

Silbervogel (Silver Bird), would have had the following characteristics:

- single-seat bomber
- wingspan: 15.0 m
- length: 28.0 m
- height: 2.10 m
- takeoff weight: 100 t
- pilot in pressurized cockpit
- designed to fly in the stratosphere
- capable of reaching any target on earth and returning to its point of origin
- retractable undercarriage
- integrated rocket engine with 100,000 kp thrust
- fuselage designed as lifting body

Diesel and liquid oxygen would fuel the rocket engine, with the fuel comprising 90% of the takeoff weight, i.e. 90 tons. This left a total of 10 tons remaining for the aircraft's empty weight and any payload.

The aircraft would take off from a 3 km long launch rail. In doing so, the *Silbervogel* would be propelled by two solid fuel booster rockets and a rocket sled, with a total thrust of 600,000 kp, accelerating the plane to a speed of 500 m/s (Mach 1.5!) before it lifted off and climbed out at an angle of 30% at a constant speed to an altitude of 1,200 meters. At that point the main engine would be switched on for a period of 8 minutes, and the aircraft would climb to an altitude of 145 km at a speed of 22,100 km/h (Mach 20). Then the airplane would continue to climb to 285 km without power, where it would glide along the earth's atmosphere in a flight profile resembling an oscillation wave, constantly rising and sinking much like a flat stone skipping across the water. Such a profile would give it a range of 20,000 km to 40,000 km, depending on the payload carried. Landing would be made like any other normal airplane, as the *Silbervogel* would be equipped with a retractable landing gear. The first stress tests of individual components took place in 1939, but the problems of supersonic flight were still a long way from being resolved, not to mention the special thermal problems spawned by hypersonic flight.

Thus Eugen Sänger continued to work on his liquid fueled rocket. As early as 1941 this offered performance results that exceeded those of the rocket motor developed by Wernher von Braun for the A4. But in 1942 the RLM killed the long-range bomber project, since there was little belief that such long term plans would have any effect whatsoever on the war's outcome. Dr. Sänger and his assistant (and later wife),

Dr. Irene Bredt, were both transferred to the DFS. The *Silbervogel* would have undoubtedly become the world's first hypersonic plane.

Within the DFS Dr. Sänger worked on developing pulse-jet engines, which would ultimately be needed for hypersonic flight as well, since they were significantly more economical to operate than rocket engines. Work on these engines had advanced so far before the war ended that a Do 217-E2 was able to carry out an airborne test with one mounted on its spine.

In 1944 Dr. Sänger once again attempted to promote his stratoglider, and submitted a memorandum to the RLM for "bombarding New York with a single free-fall bomb that would be carried in the stratoglider's fuselage between the fuel tanks." Yet again, however, the RLM showed no real interest in the idea.

After the end of the Second World War Dr. Sänger went to work at the French aeronautical research institute ONERA, and there continued his research on the theme of pulse jet propulsion. He played a major role in the development of the Nord Griffon II, which completed its maiden flight in 1957 and was equipped with a combination turbojet/pulse jet engine (unshrouded ATAR engine). By the end of this experimental program in 1959 the airplane had reached a maximum speed of Mach 2.1—a new speed record for the time.

Dr. Sänger returned to his homeland in the 1960s, when Germany renewed its interest in space travel. Again, he focused his efforts on the single-stage winged rocket powered space transports as a natural development of his original space glider design. During the years from 1962 to 1967 the Junkers and Bölkow companies undertook extensive studies in this area, on which Dr. Sänger worked up until his death in 1964. It was in this context that Dr. Sänger worked at his Research Institute for Physics of Jet Propulsion on, among other things, a hot water rocket that would accelerate a takeoff sled with space glider up to a speed of 150 meters per second. This would have offered the advantage of the space glider only requiring a lightweight undercarriage (tailored to the landing weight), rather than a heavy landing gear that would have to be designed for the much higher takeoff weight.

After the death of Eugen Sänger the German space industry shifted from single stage systems to a simpler-to-implement two stage system. By 1967 the two firms of Junkers and Bölkow had jointly developed a concept for a two stage space transporter with a takeoff mass of 200 tons. This concept was ultimately one of the two cornerstones of the American space shuttle development. Under the auspices of a NASA program the American industry carried out studies in the years 1968 and 1969 on winged space transports. Starting in 1970 the industry began, under NASA, to develop the concept of a two stage space transport with rocket propulsion and 2,000 ton takeoff weight, an idea virtually identical to the Junkers-Bölkow design of 1967. The actual development of the space shuttle began in July 1972. At the same time all further activities of NASA and the USAF on the theme of lifting bodies were terminated, to include the experiments with the X-24, M2, and HL-10 airframes.

For cost reasons the idea of a two stage concept was dropped, however, and replaced by single stage solid fuel rockets (boosters) and a jettisonable tank that contained the fuel for the main engine, which would be integrated into the shuttle itself. Because of its return to earth as a glider, the space shuttle was completely designed for reentry at hypersonic speeds. The original requirement was for a payload of 29.5 tons at an earth orbit of 350 km, with a takeoff weight of 2,025 tons.

The first flight of a space shuttle (Columbia) took place on 12 April 1981, lasting 54 hours and 2 minutes.

As early as the mid-1980s work began on a shuttle successor, both in the United States as well as in Europe. This time it would follow the path of an aerodynamic space transport with a horizontal takeoff profile, something that corresponded to Sänger's ideas.

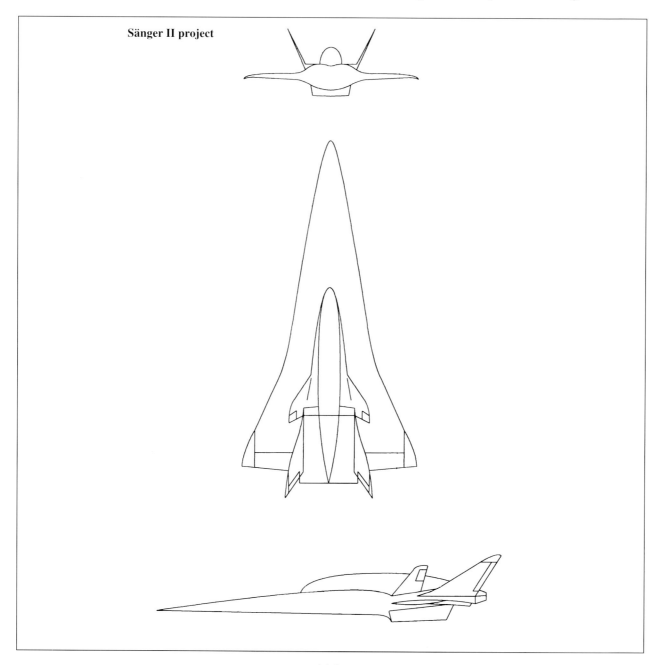

Sänger II project

114

Space Shuttle Technical Data:	
length (Orbiter)	37.24 m
length (system)	56.14 m
height (Orbiter)	17.27 m
height (system)	23.34 m
span	23.79 m
takeoff weight	2,041 t
landing weight	105.7 t
max. payload	24.9 t
thrust (booster)	14.678 kN
thrust (Orbiter)	1,752 kN

In the USA it was NASA and the Navy that began on the X-30 NASP (National Aero Space Project) in 1985, with a military objective foremost in mind. Among other things, this program explored the use of so-called scramjet propulsion as a priority. This is a type of ramjet propulsion in which the air flows through the combustion chamber at a supersonic speed, which is why it is also referred to as supersonic combustion.

From 1984 onward British Aerospace in England worked on the HOTOL (Horizontal Takeoff and Landing) project, a single stage unmanned space transport that would carry a payload of seven to eight tons in a near earth orbit and 1.3 tons in geosynchronous orbit. Takeoff weight would have been about 270 tons, of which 215 tons (translating to 79.6%) would comprise the fuel alone.

In Germany it was the Messerchmitt-Bölkow-Blohm (MBB) that involved itself with a two stage space transport concept from May 1986 onward. The first stage of this design would be a hypersonic aircraft with turbo-ramjet propulsion. It was planned to use liquid hydrogen as the fuel. This German project, which was also known as the Sänger II, envisioned the strict separation between manned and unmanned missions. For this reason there were two different upper stages designed:

- HORUS (Hypersonic Orbital Upper Stage) for manned missions with a crew of two to four astronauts and a potential payload of two to three tons
- CARGUS for unmanned missions with a payload of up to eight tons

The total takeoff weight of the two stage space transport was expected to be about 240 tons.

This two stage concept would have offered several advantages. On the one hand, the cruise capability of the ramjet propelled first stage offered the possibility of launching directly from Europe, with a cruise flight then covering several thousand kilometers to the "penetration point" into near earth or geosynchronious orbit. On the other hand, a hypersonic airliner could be developed from the first stage, since the requirement for the first stage to have a capability of a 96 ton payload carried over 3,100 km is equivalent to transporting 230 passengers over 10,500 km. The optimum cruise speed of the first stage was to have been Mach 4.4 at 26,000 meters' altitude. For separation of the upper stage, the first stage would then have accelerated to a maximum speed of Mach 6.6 at an altitude of 35,000 meters.

The primary difference between the HORUS upper stage to the space shuttle and the roughly contemporary French HERMES proposal was that HORUS itself would have carried 70 tons of fuel on board, and therefore would have possessed a true propulsion stage. The engine of the HORUS was to have operated at a combustion chamber pressure of 270 bar. Work on the Sänger II terminated in 1992.

SÄNGER Project Data (effective January 1989)

	Sänger first stage (EHTV)	upper stage HORUS
overall length	84.5 m	32.8 m
span	41.4 m	17.0 m
empty weight	149 t	22.2 t
fuel weight	100 t	65.5 t
payload weight	91 t (HORUS)	3.3 t (2-4 t)
takeoff weight	340 t	91.0 t
airspeeds:		
cruise (at 26,000 m)	Mach 4.4	
maximum (at 35,000 m)	Mach 6.6	Mach 25
propulsion	turbo ramjet engine	high pressure rocket engine
initial thrust	5 x 360 kN	1 x 1,200 kN

Sänger lower stage in comparison to a derivative hypersonic passenger aircraft:

SÄNGER first stage	passenger plane	
total takeoff weight	340 t	280 t
max. payload	96 t (upper stage)	25 t (230 passengers)
overall length	84.5 m	84.5 m
wingspan	41.4 m	41.4 m
wing area	735 m^2	735 m^2
tank volume	1,400 m^3	1,400 m^3
net weight	159 t	155 t
max. fuel weight	95 t	100 t
range	2 x 3,100 km	10,500 km

Ultra-Light
Rocket Fighter Projects

Allied bomber attacks against Germany's industry intensified considerably beginning in 1943, primarily against the heavy industries and the petrochemical facilities with their hydration works. One example of the precariousness of the situation is the raid in the spring of 1944 against the hydration works at Leuna and Pölltsch, which involved 1,000 bombers with 700 escort fighters.

It now became apparent that directing friendly fighters within the Reich often took upwards of half an hour, often with no enemy contact taking place because the Allied bomber formations would suddenly change direction at the last minute, with the German interceptors finding themselves in empty airspace, or having to turn back because of fuel shortage. It is therefore understandable that the RLM sought a way out of this predicament and, in the fall of 1944, issued a requirement for a point defense fighter that would be based in the direct proximity of the site to be protected. This point defense fighter would be small and light, as well as easy to produce, with the selection of materials and the necessary production resources not placing ongoing emergency fighter production programs in jeopardy. In addition, the requirement called for a superior climb rate and speed, allowing the point defense fighter to take off only after the enemy aircraft were virtually in visible range from the interceptor's airfield.

This requirement was issued parallel to and independent of the Me 163, which at that time was in development and production, and whose history reached back to before the war. The concept designs submitted by the individual aviation companies are examined in brief below, to include those that did not leave the drawing boards.

Junkers Ju EF 127 *Wally*

The Junkers Ju EF 127 *Wally* is a follow-on development of the EF 126 *Elly* that was developed as a competitor to the Heinkel P.1077 *Romeo* as part of the emergency fighter program. The EF1126 was conceived as an ultralight single-seat fighter. Propulsion was via an Argus pulse-jet on the fuselage's dorsal spine; additional thrust for takeoff was provided by two solid fuel RATO units. Landing took place on a single central skid. On 12 December 1944 members of the RLM viewed a mockup of the ER126. In early 1945, however, the RLM canceled the project, with one of the reasons being the Argus pulse-jet's sharp drop in performance at higher altitudes.

After the war the Soviets had a prototype of the EF126 built and tested under tow. Over the course of the program former Junkers test pilot Matthies was involved in a fatal crash of the EF126 in 1946, with the airplane itself being completely destroyed as well.

The EF127 was based on the EF126's layout, but necessitated changes in certain areas, such as the propulsion system used. An HWK 109-509 A-2 was accordingly installed in the aft fuselage, equipped with a separate primary and cruise combustion chamber. Mounting points for the two 1,000 kp RATO units were retained as before, however. Furthermore, the change from the Argus pulse-jet required a change in the rudder. The fuselage was slightly modified in order to accept the tank system for the *C-Stoff* and *T-Stoff* fuels. In addition, the central skid was replaced by a retractable tricycle undercarriage borrowed from the He 162. A mockup of the EF127 was built prior to the war's end.

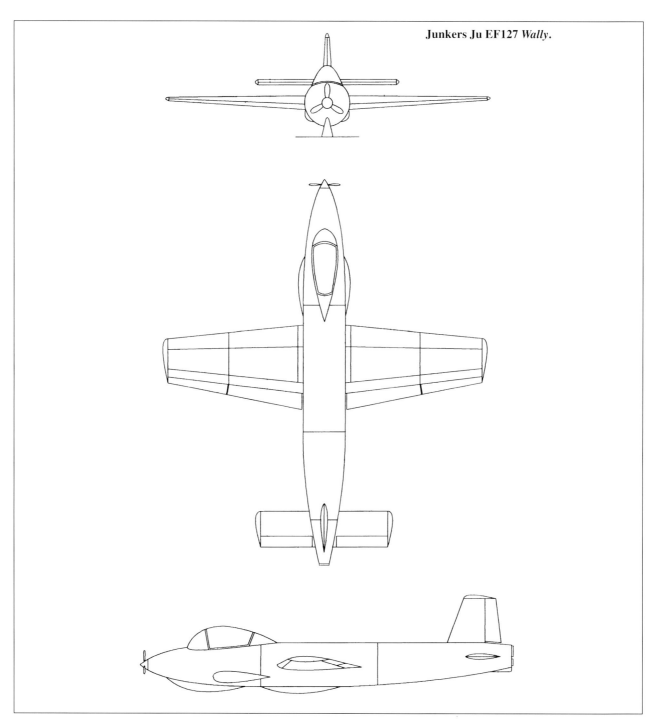

Junkers Ju EF127 *Wally*.

Arado Ar E381

A developmental contract was issued to the Arado company in the fall of 1944 for a rocket-powered miniature fighter. Its intended role was the interception of daylight bomber formations.

With this as the criterion, Arado drew up a compact rocket-powered fighter, the Ar E381. The aircraft would be carried on the standard ordnance attachment points of an Ar 234C or Ar 234D. The team would climb to an altitude of 6,000 meters, taking about eight minutes in the process. From its slightly higher vantage point the Ar E381 would be released, descending in an unpowered curved trajectory before igniting the rocket engine and engaging the enemy bombers. After its attack the pilot would immediately enter into a steep descent and land at an outlying field. To this end the Ar E381 was equipped with a braking parachute and a shock absorbing landing skid that extended prior to landing. After landing the aircraft was disassembled into its main components, put onto trucks, and returned to its home airfield.

Junkers Ju EF127 *Wally*

Role: point defense fighter

Crew: one pilot

Wings: cantilever mid-wing design. Two piece, wooden single spar wing; ailerons on outer wings and trailing edge camber flaps on the inner wings

Fuselage: all-metal monocoque fuselage with circular cross section

Control Surfaces: cantilever standard empennage of wooden construction

Undercarriage: retractable standard undercarriage

Engine: 1 x HWK 109-509 A-2 with 2000 kp total thrust, with the main combustor delivering 200-1,700 kp and the cruise combustor 300 kp; tank system with 500 kg *C-Stoff* and 1,088 kg *T-Stoff* in three fuselage tanks; optional additional fitting of two solid-fuel RATO booster rockets.

Armament: 2 x MG 151/20 or MG 213 in fuselage nose and a total of up to 12 *Panzerblitz* launch frames beneath the wings

In this configuration, performance for the EF 127 was estimated as follows:

max. speed: 950 km/h

time to climb to 10,000 m: 75 seconds

total flight time: 11 minutes 30 seconds

tactical range: 240 km

Arado Ar E381

Role: interceptor

Crew: one pilot

Wings: cantilever shoulderwing design of metal construction. Single section wing with steel tube spars, skinned with pressed steel plates and filled with foam; ailerons running the entire length of the trailing edge. Wing attached to the fuselage using quick-release bolts

Fuselage: linear, simple construction, comprising three segments: the nose of mixed-media construction, the armored cockpit and tank system, and the steel skinned tail section. Braking parachute in the fuselage center section; three (6 mm) armored plates fitted into the tail section, one behind the other, offering protection for the pilot, fuel and rocket engine.

Cockpit: pilot in the prone position, yaw controlled; side entry hatch through the armor plating (6 mm); cockpit protected fore by a fixed armor plate (6 mm) and hinged plate (20 mm) with viewport

Control Surfaces: cantilever twin rudder design, with rudders capping the horizontal stabilizer. The empennage is attached to the fuselage using quick-release bolts.

Undercarriage: central retractable and shock absorbed skid

Engine: 1 x HWK 109-509C with 400 kp cruise thrust (only the cruise combustor of the 109-509C was installed); tank system located in aft section of the armored cockpit

Armament: several rockets in the wing roots (R4M or RZ 73) and two MG 131s in the fuselage

The initial design prevented the pilot from leaving the Ar E381 once it was hung onto the Ar 234C-3. This was changed in a new design drawn up in late 1944, which called for a side-opening entry hatch for the plane.

A few all-wood trainer versions of the Ar E381 were supposedly completed before the war's end. Whether or not they were actually tested is not known and is highly doubtful.

Messerschmitt Me P1104

This rocket-powered point defense fighter was designed with a conventional mid-wing layout, borrowing the wings from the FZG 76 (another designation for the Fi 103, or V1). This had a rectangular planform and flaps running the entire length of the wing's trailing edge. The empennage also had a rectangular planform. With the exception of the forward fuselage the entire aircraft was to have been made of wood, with

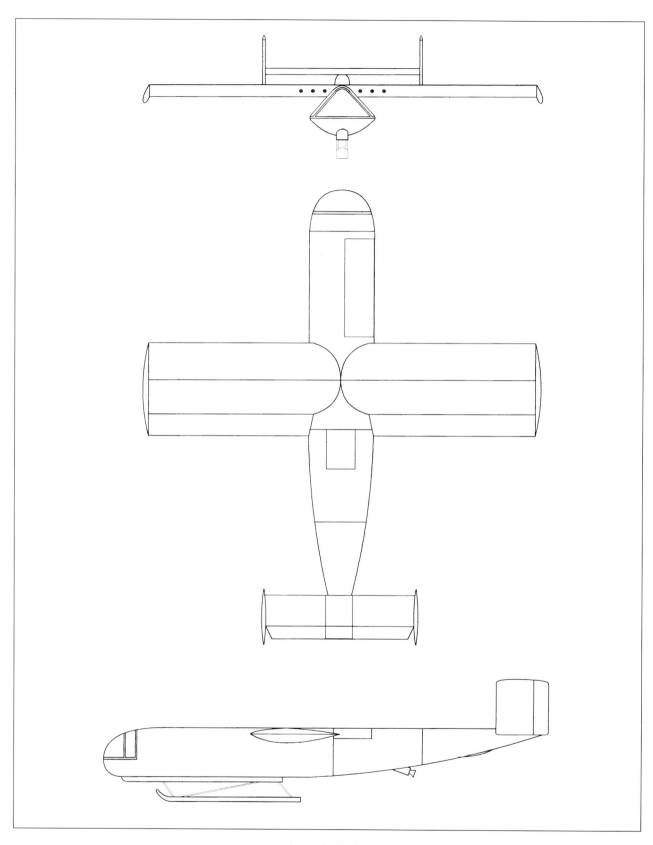

Arado Ar E 381

construction so simplified that it could be accomplished with the most basic of tools. The forward fuselage was designed to be an armored box in which the pilot sat. So that the pilot would have a good all-round view the canopy was set atop the fuselage. An extendable underfuselage skid was planned for landing to save the weight of a proper landing gear. Propulsion was intended to be the HWK 109-509 A-2 with a total thrust of 2,000 kp.

The project was canceled in the wake of the RLM's decision in favor of the Bachem BP20.

The Bachem BP20 and the Heinkel He P.1077 *Julia* were also offered to the RLM under the point defense fighter request for tender. Since, however, these designs have been discussed in detail elsewhere, no further mention is necessary here.

In addition, there was a handful of other plans for ultralight rocket-powered fighters that, for the most part, were developed and offered to the RLM independently within the industry. These included the parasite and *Rammjäger* projects by DFS and from Messerschmitt.

The parasite, or towed fighters, were miniature fighters that were either towed or carried suspended from a mother plane to altitude to within range of the enemy aircraft. Tow or mother aircraft included the Bf 109, Fw 190, or Ar 234.

An important criterion for these miniature fighters was that they could be produced simply in large quantities.

DFS *Eber*

The *Eber* project was carried out by the DFS in conjunction with the RLM's research department. This program involved a disposable aircraft designed for a two-time attack against enemy airplanes. It was planned that the airplane would be towed to altitude to within 2,000 meters of an enemy formation by either an Fw 190 or an Me 262. Two variants were studied for different attack profiles: ramming and firing. For the ramming profile, the pilot was expected to ram the enemy airplane with a speed advantage of about 200 km/h, causing it to crash. The pilot would be protected by an armored tub. Extensive research into the impact of the two aircraft, however, revealed that such a collision would result in acceleration up to 100 g (100 times the force of gravity), and the profile was quickly abandoned. The firing profile involved the pilot, on his initial pass against the enemy airplane, attacking from astern in a high speed glide, then igniting his

rocket engine after passing the enemy in order to set up for another firing pass against the same or another aircraft, with enough power to carry out a second attack. Following the attack, it was planned that the pilot would separate from the enemy and then bail out, drifting safely to the ground. The aircraft itself would be destroyed.

This operational profile meant that the pilots would neither be expected to take off or to land, and would therefore only require training in carrying out firing approaches. Planned armament included either an MK 108 or unguided R4M rockets.

Messerschmitt Me P1103

Messerschmitt began working on the P1103 project in July 1944. This was a *Rammjäger* with massive nose armor. This involved six armor plates, one behind the other, in the nose of the airplane, which was expected to weigh just 1,100 kg. The fuselage had a width of only 0.79 m to offer as narrow a silhouette from the front as possible. The pilot was housed in the cockpit in a prone position in order to better withstand the acceleration forces on impact. Following a successful attack, the pilot would be pulled from the aircraft via parachute after the nose section had separated. The airframe would drift to earth on a 'chute as well for possible reuse. The P1103 was to have been carried to altitude under tow, whereupon the four RI-502 solid fuel rockets (each with a thrust of 1,000 kp) would be ignited, and the airplane would accelerate under its own power, while at the same time climbing to a higher altitude. Armament was to have been two MK 108s with 30 rounds of ammunition each, housed on either side of the pilot in the lower fuselage, as well as a *Nebelwerfer* (21 cm caliber), also in the lower fuselage. The wings would have come from the FZG 76.

An on-board fighter variant was also conceived for the P1103, in which the pilot would be housed in a seated position. This fighter was to only have been armed with a single MK 108 carried beneath the pilot's seat.

All these projects, which amounted to nothing more than a desperate act of Germany's aviation industry against the seemingly endless waves of Allied bombers, were ultimately dropped—most likely due to the fact that there was really very little faith in what were, in part, still quite exotic designs. Instead, preference was given to the proven types, such as the Me 262 A-1a and the He 162 A-1/A-2, both of which had the added advantage of being in large scale production.

The theoretical data for the two aircraft were as follows:		
	Type I	Type II
wing area	36.5 m²	43.0 m²
takeoff weight	10,000 kg	13,500 kg
gross weight	5,620 kg	5,930 kg
landing weight	4,220 kg	4,950 kg
climb thrust	15,000 kp	20,000 kp
cruise thrust	900 kp	775 kp
max. speed at 2,000 m	830 km/h	830 km/h

Fieseler Fi 166

Independent of the efforts mentioned above, in 1941 the Fieseler Works carried out preliminary studies for the development of a rocket-powered fighter. Two versions were designed, which differed in areas other than just the propulsion system. This was, on the one hand, the *Höhenjäger I* (type R.R.Fl), with pure rocket propulsion offering a flight time of five minutes at an altitude of 12,000 meters. The *Höhenjäger II* (type TL-R-R-uR) was an airplane consisting of two separate components. The aircraft itself was fitted with two turbojet engines mounted beneath the wings. A rocket engine was carried in a separate fuselage together with its special tanks, and hung beneath the aft section of the actual airplane. This mixed propulsion configuration would supposedly have offered a flight time of 45 minutes at an altitude of 12,000 meters.

Rocket Engines

Rocket propulsion systems are divided according to type and consistency of the fuel used into solid fuel and liquid fuel engines.

Solid fuel Rockets

A characteristic feature of solid fuel rockets is that the fuel tank and combustion chamber are one and the same. The fuel, a mixture of an oxidizer substance and a combustible component, is contained within the combustion chamber. The fuel is also relatively stable, even non-reactive, at normal room temperature and atmospheric pressure. To be sure, a quality that makes the storage of solid fuel rockets easier and less dangerous, but at the same time means that an ignitor is required to initiate a reaction (start the engine). This ultimately causes pressure in the combustion chamber to build up from 50 to 150 *bar*. This condition is one reason why the weight of early combustion chambers was often more than the weight of the fuel content they held. Once ignited, the combustion process cannot be stopped.

Another important characteristic of solid fuel rockets is that the resulting thrust is directly related to the size of the combusting fuel surface and the rate of combustion. Therefore, it is possible to affect the resulting thrust by the shape of the fuel composition. In short, this means that the rougher the surface the greater the resulting thrust. An important criterion for such systems is that the resulting thrust be constant for the entire burn time. This can be achieved by a special design of the combustion chamber, spawning such options as an internal combustor, a radial combustor, and many other possibilities. A major problem, however, is ensuring adequate cooling for the combustion chamber's walls.

The first solid fuel rockets were powder driven, which made use of black powder as fuel. However, since the exhaust nozzles were not designed for the exhaust gas, they only offered speeds of about 1,000 meters per second. It was not until the use of smokeless powder (a mixture of nitro-glycerin and nitro-cellulose) and specially designed nozzles—so called Laval nozzles (borrowed from steam turbine construction)—that speeds of 2,000 meters per second were possible.

The solid fuel rockets used in the Second World War offered a constant level of thrust for the most part. It wasn't until around the end of the war that solid fuel rockets were manufactured that were capable of producing varying levels of thrust, as with the engine for the HS 298, for example.

Because of the short burn time of solid fuel rockets, as a rule even today this type is used for short bursts of propulsion, such as for the American space shuttle's boosters and the European Ariane 4 cargo rocket. Even when the fuel substance used today is different than that used earlier. Today, the oxidizer is more likely to be materials such as ammonium perchlorate, lithium perchlorate, or ammonium nitrate. Possible fuels include all solid hydrocarbons, organic plastics, vinyl polyester, and other substances.

Liquid fuel Rockets

The Russian Ziolkovski was the first to work on development of the liquid fuel rocket, around the end of the 19th century. Even then he recommended the use of pure oxygen and hydrogen as fuels because of the high amount of energy they released. With liquid fuel rockets the fuel tanks and combustion chamber are separate, and can therefore be optimally tailored to given requirements. This advantage predestines such systems as long-term propulsion options. Furthermore, liquid fuel offered a significantly greater thrust yield over solid fuels.

Yet even with liquid fuel systems there are several problems with no easy solutions. For example, the precise combination of fuel has to be selected from among the enormous amount of options, with cryogenic liquids (liquified gases) additionally requiring insulation. The use as a long-burn propulsion means that the combustion chamber and nozzle walls require cooling. In addition, the fuels must be pumped into the combustion chamber from the tanks in order to maintain the high pressure within the combustion chamber. And last but not least, the majority of fuel combinations require ignition.

The problem of combustion chamber cooling was solved by Eugen Sänger, among others, by his development of regenerative cooling. This involves a fuel component being pumped through fuel lines located within the walls of the combustion chamber and Laval nozzle prior to entering the combustion chamber. This principle is still used for today's ultramodern rocket systems.

Depending on the oxidizer used, liquid fuel rockets can be classified into three different categories. Rocket engines using hydrogen peroxide (H_2O_2), engines using liquid oxygen (LOX), and those operating on nitric acid (HNO_3). Of these, hydrogen peroxide is the only oxidator that adds to the resulting thrust, as it releases energy while breaking down. The available oxygen composition, however, is less than that for the other two substances, and producing it is more expensive, as well. In Germany it was Helmuth Walter in Kiel who chiefly used this oxidizer in his rocket engines.

Liquid oxygen is the ideal oxidizer and, in addition, is relatively inexpensive to produce. On the other hand, it has a low storage life (continuous evaporation) and a very low boiling point of -182.97% C. The German Walter Thiel used this oxidizer in Peenemünde as part of his long range rocket program.

Nitrogen oxide is the most cost effective and most widely available oxidizer. Concentrated nitrogen oxide, however, is extremely aggressive and attacks almost every known metal. This aggression in relation to steel can be reduced by adding phosphoric acid, and by adding sulphuric acid to the mix it is possible to improve the ignition capabilities. Germany's Helmut von Zborowski worked with nitrogen oxide at BMW as an oxidizer.

For fuel, virtually all known fuel organic compounds can be used. These include:

- gasoline and its derivatives
- alcohol
- petroleum
- benzene derivatives

In order to avoid additional complications with the engines it was preferred to use fuel that spontaneously reacted with the oxidizer due to its chemical qualities, i.e. without external initial ignition. Such fuel combinations are called hypergol.

A key concern with liquid fuel rocket propulsion systems is the manner in which the fuels are fed into the combustion chamber so as to maintain the necessary high pressure within the chamber. There are two different methods: pressurized gas feed and pump feed. With pressurized gas, the fuel tanks are fed compressed air that is either carried in separate tanks nor generated on board. The disadvantage to this method is that the fuel tanks must be able to withstand the enormous amount of excess pressure (about 5 to 10 *bar* above the combustion chamber's pressure of 20 *bar*) caused by the combustion chamber pressure and the pressure loss in the fuel lines from the fuel tank to the combustion chamber. As a result, pressurized gas feed is best suited for short-burn propulsion systems, or for a low fuel flow rate over a long period.

Designation	Composition
A-Stoff	liquid oxygen
B-Stoff	hydrazine hydrate (catalyst for hydrogen peroxide and methanol reactions)
Br-Stoff	gasoline (non-refined benzine)
C-Stoff	30% hydrazine hydrate, 57% methanol, 13% water with potassium cuprocyanide amounts
M-Stoff	methanol
R-Stoff	*Tonka* (organic amino mixtures of basic character), identified in the following compositions:
Tonka 93	(20% non-refined xylidine F, 20% aniline M, 20% ethylanifine, 20% isquexylamine, 10% benzol)
Tonka 250	(50% non-refined xylidine F, 50% triethylaminea)
Tonka 500	(12% non-refined xylidine F 15% aniline, 22% monomethylanilinea, 21% triethylamine, 16% benzol and 14% benzine solution)
S-Stoff	*Salbei* (96% nitric acid and 4% ferrous chloride)
SV-Stoff	*Salbei* (90-98% gaseous nitric acid, 2-10% nitrogen dioxide)
Z-Stoff	Watery solution of sodium or calcium
Visol	Divinyisobutyl acid ester; together with nitric acid forms a spontaneously reacting hypergol
Diglycol	Diglycol nitrate; a liquid poured powder propellant (solid fuel rocket)

Pump feed is particularly suited for high fuel flow rates and/or long burn times. It involves two centrifugal pumps (one per fuel component) driven by a steam turbine, which in turn is powered by a mixture of heated steam and oxygen. This mixture can, for example, be drawn from the catalytic breakup of hydrogen peroxide in a separate steam generator. In this case, particular care must be taken with the compression of the combined wave from the steam turbine and the two attached centrifugal pumps to avoid any contact whatsoever between the two fuel components, an event that would trigger an uncontrollable reaction.

At quite an early stage, to disguise the programs and keep them secret the RLM issued identification number 109, with suffixes possible from 500 to 999, to differentiate between the turbojet engines (also identified by the number 109). Issuance of the suffixes was initially made in chronological order. Later these were reserved for individual companies in order to make classification easier.

However, by the war's final stages it was no longer possible to properly classify all rocket engine developments.

The RLM also issued cover designations for the different rocket fuels and special components.

Because of the large number of rocket propulsion systems developed, only those that were integrated into airframes or used for boosting takeoffs will be discussed below. To round out the picture, the remaining rocket motors—primarily used as propulsion for diverse flying bodies—are listed in the table on pages 148/149. No claim is made for the table's completeness, however.

Company	End numbers	
WASAG	2	(512, 522,...)
Schmidding	3	(513, 533,...)
Rheinmetall	5	(505, 515,...)
BMW	8	(548, 558,...)
HWK	9	(509, 559, 729)

Hellmuth Walter Kommanditgesellschaft (HWK)

During the time from 1930 to 1936 chemist Hellmuth Walter, at the Krupp-Germaniawerft in Kiel, developed a gas turbine for ships under contract from the Naval Office. With no knowledge of the ongoing efforts to develop a liquid fuel rocket at the Kummersdorf test center, there was born the idea of using such propulsion for underwater systems (torpedoes), with the unique problem here being able to operate independent of an external oxygen source. As a result, Walter began searching for a suitable oxidizer, which he found in the form of hydrogen peroxide (H_2O_2), also later known as *T-Stoff*. However, at this early date it could only be produced in small concentrations (up to a maximum of 35%). Hellmuth Walter had the idea of catalytically breaking down hydrogen peroxide into oxygen and heated steam and using the released energy for generating thrust. The so called "cold-Walter method" was born. Due mainly to its simplicity and relatively low operating temperature, this method was easy to put into practice.

Large amounts of energy are needed to produce hydrogen peroxide from water, which releases relatively unstable hydrogen peroxide in the form of heat as it breaks down. For this, a minimum of 65% hydrogen peroxide is necessary, since only oxygen and hot water are generated at lower concentrations. The optimal accumulative concentration is between 80 and 85%, ensuring that the resulting water is completely turned to steam, and the resulting oxygen-seam mixture reaches a temperature of 460% C. Technologically, higher concentrations could not be produced, as they are exceptionally prone to explosion and solidify even in a light frost when compared to weaker concentrations. Breakdown of hydrogen peroxide is accomplished by the use of catalysts. Chief among these are natrium-, calcium-, and potassium permanganate, which can be employed either as crystal, a watery solution, or by soaking into a porous carrier material (pumice stone).

Together with Dr. Albert Pietzsch at the Electrochemical Works at Höllriegelskreuth, near Munich, Walter succeeded in finding a way for major industrial production of highly concentrated hydrogen peroxide. For this purpose a plant was built at Lauterberg, in the Harz Mountains, with a yearly output of 15,000 tons of high concentration hydrogen peroxide, which began production in 1940. In addition, suitable materials for the tanks and fuel systems were discovered that could withstand the aggressive nature of hydrogen peroxide. It was found that tanks made of pure aluminum or aluminum alloys free of copper were suitable, although these had to be treated by eloxadizing, waxing, and applying oxine (a liquid solution made from preparation 177, sodium hydroxide, and perhydrol. Also suitable were chrome plated steel, nickel, ceramic, and glass. With glass, however, the tanks had to be darkened or coated with a light eliminating layer, as sunlight causes hydrogen peroxide to break down. For the seals, tubes, and tank linings the synthetic materials igelite and mipolam (product name for polyvinylchloride) were used.

The path was then clear for developing an aircraft propulsion system using hydrogen peroxide. The design for a rocket engine was submitted in 1934 that was based on the principle of the catalytic breakdown of highly concentrated hydrogen peroxide described above. For this, Walter initially planned to use lead as the catalyst.

The DVL learned of these efforts and showed interest. It contracted with Hellmuth Walter for the development of a rocket propulsion system having a thrust of 400 kp to be used in aircraft.

On 1 July 1935 Hellmuth Walter established the "Ingenierbüro H. Walter GmbH," which was first housed in private quarters. As early as the fall of 1935 successful tests of the rocket system were carried out at the site of the Navy's physics and chemical test center at Kiel-Dietrichsdorf on a provisional test bench. For these tests, Walter selected natrium permanganate for the catalyst, which was contained in the combustion chamber in a gelatinous form. Using compressed air, the hydrogen peroxide was misted onto this gelatin mass via spray jets. At first, the system developed a thrust of 100 kp, although this was successively increased to 300 kp. In 1936 this rocket motor eventually produced a thrust of 1,000 kp. From this system Walter developed a rocket engine with a thrust of about 130 kp and a burn time of 45 seconds, making practical flight testing possible. The system was handed over to the DVL in 1936, and there tested in flight as a takeoff booster on a Heinkel He 72 *Kadett*. First flight of the He 72 thus equipped was in January 1937 at Ahlimbsmühle, with Dr. Pleines at the controls. This was the first flight of a liquid fuel rocket in Germany. That same year an improved variant became available, the HWK RI, which made use of potassium permanganate (*Z-Stoff*) injected in liquified form into the combustion chamber as a catalyst. This dramatically improved the engine's controllability, and the resulting thrust rose to 290 kp with a burn time of 30 seconds. This rocket engine was tested in a Focke-Wulf Fw 56 *Stösser* in the summer of 1937, with the integration of the rocket engine into the airframe again being accomplished by the Heinkel Company. By swapping out the exhaust nozzle, the maximum thrust of the engine could be alternated between 10, 200, and 290 kp. A considerable number of flights had taken place by the summer of 1939 (full-throttle level flights, banking turns, and takeoff trials) using this modified Fw 56, with marked improvements in the aircraft's flight performance (particularly its climb rate) being noted.

Thrust, which lasted a maximum of 30 seconds before the fuel ran out, could not be regulated on this first rocket propulsion system. The catalyst was in a mash form inside the combustion chamber, which meant that after every operation the complete system had to be disassembled and thoroughly cleaned out.

This rocket system was also installed in a governable version with 400 kp thrust in the DFS 194.

In the meantime, Walter and his company had moved onto the site of an abandoned gas works, where he had special test benches built.

After being successfully tested, the HWK RI (HWK *Rakete 1*) was developed by Walter into the HWK RI-203, which was then fitted in the Heinkel He 176. For the RI-203, methanol (*M-Stoff*) was used in place of a catalyst, with methanol reacting spontaneously with hydrogen peroxide. Another significant improvement over the first engine was the use of turbopumps to feed the fuels, enabling a major improvement in thrust control. Power for these turbopumps was provided by a combined steam turbine (discussed in detail earlier in this section), which in turn was fed by its own steam generator (*T-* and *Z-Stoff*). This engine supplied a maximum thrust of 600 kp with a burn time of 60 seconds.

With the RI system as a basis, Walter developed a jettisonable rocket booster (109-500) for heavily laden aircraft, which had a burn time of 30 seconds and a thrust of 500 kp. The system carried 155 kg of hydrogen peroxide that, like the catalyst, was pumped into the combustion chamber using pressurized air. After burning out, the booster was released and drifted to the ground beneath its own parachute, where it was recovered. This simple and robust device could be used over and over again. Because of its external design it was also known as the *Kraftei* (power egg). Testing on various kinds of airplanes began at Neuhardenberg in 1937, even before the flight of the He 112R, and field/production testing continued in the summer of 1938 at Peenemünde-West, where it terminated in 1939. For these tests, Heinkel provided first one, then an additional He 111, which carried the booster engines beneath each outer wing. The initial phase of testing included bench run-ups that primarily served to study the functional safety of the rocket systems and the reliability of the attachment points on the aircraft. Once these had been completed satisfactorily, the first takeoff of an He 111 carrying two booster rockets occurred. The pilots were Erich Warsitz and Walter Künzel. They first climbed to an altitude of 1,000 meters, where they throttled back on their speed before igniting the boosters. This first flight in Neuhardenberg was followed by over 100 other test flights using Walter rocket boosters. From the He 111 were derived subsequent performance requirements for rocket boosters. These required that, with a takeoff weight of 10 metric tons and with support of rocket boosters, the aircraft must reach an altitude of 20 meters after a takeoff run of 600 meters. Over the course of testing, the following takeoff procedures were formalized for an He 111 with rocket assisted takeoff (RATO) boosters:

-   takeoff into the wind with piston engines only
-   after a run of 20 to 40 meters rockets are ignited
-   rotation after a further 400 meters run
-   an altitude of 20-50 meters attained after a total takeoff run of 600 meters, at which time the RATO boosters had burned out and the aircraft dropped 2-3 meters as a result of the loss in thrust
-   level flight for 1,000 meters to build up speed

Parallel to the efforts at Neuhardenberg, research was also done into the use of RATO boosters for flying boats in 1937 off the Zingst peninsula on the Pomeranian coast. For these tests, a Do 18 flown by pilots Conrad and Schuster served as the testbed. Two HWK 109-500 RATO pods were attached to the fuselage. The unique problem with flying boats is that the aircraft must have "stepped up" on the water by the time the RATO boosters have burned out. The trials were successful, but it is unknown whether a flying boat ever flew operationally with RATO boosters. The aircraft recovery ship *Greif* from the Travemünde test center served as the focal point for the trials.

As early as 1939 an internal testing detachment (designated *Lehrstab-S*) was established at Giebelstadt under *Hptm* Mattenklott, with the goal of providing training for operational field use. Production took place at the Heinkel Works at Jenbach, in the Tyrol, and the first units were supplied to the *Luftwaffe* in mid-1940. The *Luftwaffe* had problems with these units at the outset. Since they did not have an automatic shut-off, a failure of one of the boosters meant that the airplane immediately began veering, forcing the pilot to cor-

HWK RI-203 in the DFS 194. (photo: Radinger)

128

rect. Intensive training of the operational pilots by Erich Warsitz, among others, offered rapid relief. The HWK 109-500 RATO booster clearly proved its effectiveness in over 3,000 missions on a wide variety of aircraft (He 111, Do 18, Ju 88, Me 321, etc.) during the war years.

Nevertheless, this thrust was insufficient for many types of operational profiles, and a more powerful version (109-501) was developed. This had the same design as the 109-500, was also jettisonable and reusable, and was approximately 400 mm longer. In place of the cold method, however, the so-called "hot Walter" method was employed. This involved oxygen, released by the breakdown of the hydrogen peroxide, being burned in conjunction with the fuel. Potential fuels included benzine, hydrocarbons, or hydrazine hydrate, with the latter reacting spontaneously with hydrogen peroxide and dispensing with the need for an independent catalyst. This gave the unit a thrust of 1,500 kp with a burn time of 30 seconds. The unit held 2020 kg of hydrogen peroxide, 20 kg of petroleum, 12 kg of catalyst solution, and 2 kg of compressed air, the lat-

ter being to feed the fuel. Only a few of these booster rockets were built and tested in 1942 at Peenemünde-West on various bomber types. Other than its use on the He 111Z for towing the Me 321, no other operational use in the field is known. The HWK 109-501 made use of automatic shut-off, which automatically shut down the second booster (on the other wing) in the event a single RATO booster failed.

The HWK 109-503 was derived from the 109-501 and delivered a thrust of 1,000 kp for 45 seconds.

Together with Rheinmetall, HWK also developed the 109-502 rocket motor in the years 1944/45 based on the 109-501 booster. It had the same performance as the -501, but was specially dimensioned to fit into the E1 test prototype of the *Enzian* surface-to-air missile.

The RI-203, which had proven so effective in the He 176, served as the basis for Walter's RII-203 rocket engine. This version also made use of turbopumps for fuel feed, but reverted back to hydrogen peroxide/Z-*Stoff* for its fuel combination, meaning that it operated using the cold method. The mixture of the two fuels was regulated by means of a piston manometer.

HWK RI-203 during a test run-up. (photo: Radinger)

From the RI-203 Walter developed what was probably the most successful German liquid fuel rocket motor of all time, the 109-509. This rocket propulsion system was installed as a complete unit into an airframe and consisted of an almost cuboid frame that encompassed all auxiliary systems (fuel pumps, steam generator, control and governor valves, etc.), a combustion chamber, and a linking tube between the two. In addition to a simple construction design, this layout permitted the combustion chamber to be fitted into the aircraft's aft section, with the engine framework being positioned near the aircraft's center of gravity. Methanol as a fuel was, as it became available, replaced by *C-Stoff* which, when combined with hydrogen peroxide, formed a hypergolic mixture. As with earlier versions, fuel was fed via turbopumps driven by a gas turbine that was, in turn, powered by a separate steam generator running on *T-* and *Z-Stoff*. Different variants of this propulsion system were used until 1945 in the Me 163 B and other rocket-powered aircraft.

Beginning in 1943 the HWK also began developing a rocket motor using nitric acid as the oxidizer, since nitric acid was about 100 times cheaper to produce than hydrogen peroxide. The fuel was fed into the combustion chamber using compressed air. The system supplied an initial thrust of 375 kp that dropped off to 60 kp after a 10 second burn time, then continued to burn for another 60 seconds. This sytem (109-729) did not reach production status before the war's end, however.

By 1939 employment at the company, now called simply HWK, had risen to over 300 personnel. As a result, the decision was made to set up a new plant for 1,000 employees on the Baltic-North Sea Canal. This site was completed in 1942, but by that time it was already too small. Because of the war's situation, the HWK company dispersed to five different locations, with the final assembly of the rocket motors sited in a road tunnel near Achensee in 1944. Near the end of the war there were 5,000 people working for HWK, including 300 engineers.

The Allies showed considerable interest in the Walter engines, so much so that after the war testing continued at the main site at Kiel. It lasted until the entire plant at Kiel was taken apart and shipped off, a fate that also befell the company's other sites in the eastern zone of occupation.

After the war Hellmuth Walter continued his work, first in England, then moved to the U.S. in 1950.

109-509 A-0	pre-production version for the Me 163 B from May 1943 onward with a 300-1,500 kp controllable thrust
109-509 A-1	production version for the Me 163 B from August 1944 onward as well as the propulsion system for the DFS 228 and prototypes of the Ba 349 with a 100-1,600 kp controllable thrust
109-509 A-2	version with additional cruise combustion chamber of 300 kp thrust; the main combustor offered controllable thrust from 200-1,700 kp; installation-ready from August 1944; used in the Me 163C and was intended for the Heinkel P.1077 *Julia*, among others.
109-509 B	more powerful version of the 109-509 A-1 with a controllable thrust from 100 to 2,000 kp for the Me 163 B-1; installation-ready from March 1944
109-509 C	more powerful version of the 109-509 A02 for integration into the Me 263/Ju 248; the main combustion chamber offered controllable thrust varying from 400 to 2,000 kp and the cruise combustor an additional 400 kp; installation-ready from August 1944
109-509 D	special derivative of the 109-509 C for installation in the Bachem Ba 349B; installation-ready in 1945
109-509 S	special derivative (minus the cruise combustor) of the 109-509 A-2 for installation in the DFS 228
109-559	radically simplified version of the 109-509 A-1 for installation in the Bachem Ba 349A with a controllable thrust of 150 to 1,700 kp; installation-ready from August 1944.

Wernher von Braun
Heereswaffenamt

Wernher von Braun's development of his liquid fueled A1 rocket engine at the Army Test Center in Kummserdorf ultimately led to the Heinkel He 112R, and since this was discussed in detail in the section on the He 112R it will not be repeated here.

Based on this work, Wernher von Braun began working on the development of a jettisonable rocket booster at Kummersdorf that would also be a gondola-shaped, self-contained unit kitted out with a parachute. Work on this project continued after the Army Test Center moved from Kummersdorf to Peenemünde East. Liquid oxygen and alcohol were to again serve as the fuels, which would be fed into the combustion chamber using compressed air. The engine was ignited electronically by the pilot and could be shut down at any time. Units were planned and, in part, tested with a thrust of 1,000 kp, 1,500 kp, 2,000 kp, and 2,500 kp. Among other types, these boosters were intended for use on the Junkers Ju 88 and Heinkel He 177. The system entered testing as the B8a or RI-101 and delivered 1,000 kp of thrust for 30 seconds. Practical flight testing of the booster with the first drop of a mockup was undertaken using a Heinkel He 111 at Peenemünde West on 28 August 1940. But one of the problems with this system quickly became apparent: even at a drop velocity of just 6 meters per second the booster's structure suffered lingering deformations on impact with the ground.

The program was eventually canceled, one of the reasons being due to the fact that supplying operational units with liquid oxygen would have been quite problematic.

BMW

In early 1939 the RLM issued the Brandenburgische otorenwerke GmbH, Berlin-Spandau (BRAMO) a contract for developing a liquid fuel rocket motor for military applications. This was done for two reasons, one being to offer HWK some competition, and the other being the fact that liquid fuel rockets seemed quite promising and should therefore have been explored in a systematic way. The result was that around BRAMO Berlin-Spandau there grew a relatively large developmental site with laboratories and test benches. Work subsequently began on basic development of a combustion chamber for burning liquid oxygen. Other general systems studies were also carried out there.

On 8 June 1939 the BMW Flugmotorenbau GmbH, Munich, inherited the BRAMO division of the Siemens Company, and on 1 July 1939 renamed the company as the BMW Flugmotorenwerke Brandenburg GmbH.

In the fall of 1939 the RLM tasked it with developing a RATO booster for overloaded takeoffs of transport and bomber aircraft, as well as relaunches of landed transport gliders. This system was given the designation BMW P-3370. Design was completed by the beginning of 1940. The oxidizer was intended to be 50% hydrogen peroxide, and a methanol mixture would provide the fuel. Completion of the first full prototype model took until the fall of that year due to a lack of plant resources. In addition, because of the noise it was impossible to carry out any test bench trials at the Berlin-Spandau works, and at the prompting of the RLM the company built its own test benches at the Berlin-Zühlsdorf site. The first successful ignition and burn tests using the combustion chamber took place in the autumn of 1940. But the acquisition of sufficient quantities of high concentrate hydrogen peroxide proved to be quite difficult for BMW. Efforts were therefore made to find an alternative to the hydrogen peroxide. It was for this reason that BMW researched over 3,000 different fuel combinations, either theoretically or in the laboratory. Ultimately, it was decided to make use of concentrated nitric acid (HNO_3 (*S-/Sv-Stoff*)) as the oxidizer for all further rocket engine developments at BMW. This is a yellowish, quite aggressive liquid that is quite dangerous for humans to breathe in or even touch. It was planned to use methanol as the combustible, but since it does not react with nitric acid of its own accord an initial ignition would be necessary. First combustion trials using electronic ignition around the end of 1940 were not successful. The tests of the model combustion chamber went successfully after switching to pyrotechnical ignition, however. At the same time, the search was on for a fuel that reacted more easily with nitric acid, and such a fuel was found in the form of a substance known as *Tonka*. The P-3370 was subsequently developed into the P-3372 rocket motor, which made use of the self-reacting (hypergolic) fuel combination of nitric acid and *Tonka*.

In order to feed the fuel into the combustion chamber, in 1940 BMW developed the differential piston principle, a variant of the pressurized gas method. The principle separated the cooled pressurized gas, either from an outside source or generated by the motor itself, using a free piston that had two different sized large head plates, so that different pressure was applied on both sides of the piston. A test system for experimenting with this method was completed in 1941.

In 1952 the BMW Flugmotorenwerke Berlin and Munich merged at the Munich Allach Works so that all development of aviation engines could be concentrated at one site. Rocket development was located at the southern end of the plant. The company had new test benches, assembly areas, and test shops built for the move, as well as nitric acid and *Tonka* storage facilities. The move from Berlin to Munich-Allach took place in the fall of 1942.

In October 1942 the RLM issued a contract to BMW under the heading of 109-510 for the development of a rocket engine to power the Me 163 B. Internally, BMW carried this project as the P-3390A. The engine's thrust was expected to be controllable between 300 and 1,500 kp with a burn time of 33 to 90 seconds. Series production totaling 110 units began, but

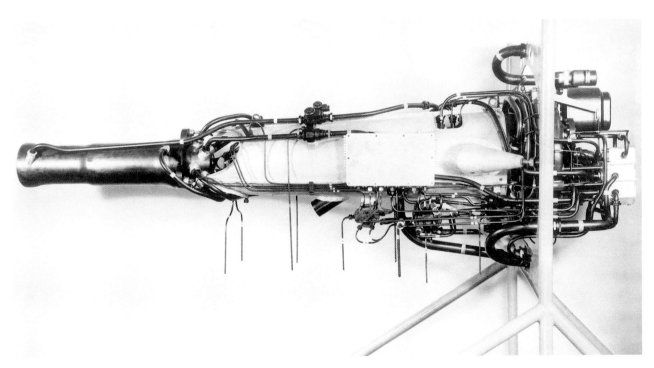

BMW Project P 3390A rocket engine for the Me 163 B.

133

in 1944 this was broken off. Fuel was a mixture of nitric acid (*Sv-Stoff*) and methanol at a ration of 1:2, fed into the combustion chamber via turbopumps. The turbopumps were driven by a single turbine that, for its part, was powered by steam from a small combustion chamber, with the steam being cooled from its initial 2,300°C to 600°C by means of water injection. This feed method was used on the P-3390 and P-3395 projects. For the other rocket engines, either compressed air or the differential piston methods were used.

Under the RLM designation 109-708 (BMW designation P-3390 and P-3391), BMW designed a rocket engine for the Me 163C that consisted of a main combustion chamber and a cruise chamber. The complete unit delivered a controllable thrust between 600 and 2,500 kp with a burn time of 35 seconds, with the cruise engine controllable between 100 and 500 kp. The *Sv-Stoff* and *Tonka* fuels were fed into the chamber via

turbopumps at a ratio of 1:3.5. Assembly of the components got underway before the war ended, and a few individual examples of completed engine units were even built.

Probably the most remarkable design for a rocket system at BMW was the engine with the RLM designation 109-718. The BMW company listed this rocket engine as the P-3395. This system was designed beginning in August 1943 specifically for a supplemental propulsion system to be adapted to the BMW 003 A-1 turbojet engine. Among other things, this manifested itself in the use of the turbojet driving the fuel pumps of the rocket motor. The first test run-up of a complete unit took place in March 1944. By mid-May of 1944 the type had been cleared for flight testing, once the following data had been established with a test of the prototype combustion chamber in April 1944:

BMW 109-003R, a turbine rocket engine for the Me 262 C-2 S.

run time: 15 runs at 3 minutes
thrust: 1,000 kp constant

The rocket engine itself provided a thrust of 1,250 kp for a maximum of three minutes, and with the turbojet the combined thrust offered by the BMW 003 TLR was 2,050 kp. The fuel again was a mixture of *Sv-Stoff* and *Tonka* at a ratio of 1:3.5. This propulsion system had been developed especially for the Me 262 C-2b interceptor. The Me 262 V074 testbed took off on 26 March 1945 at Lechfeld on its first flight with its rocket engine switched on. The second and final flight took place just three days later.

For protective reasons, rocket assembly moved from Munich-Allach to Bruckmühl, near Bad Aibling. When the Allies occupied the Munich facilities in April 1945 they discovered four rocket projects still being worked on.

Between 1940 and 1945 BMW completed a total of 1,700 experimental and production rocket engines. Yet only a handful of projects actually reached production maturity, of which none actually became operational, however. The reasons for this may have been that there wasn't enough time to deal with all the technical problems, and that BMW was pursuing too many projects at the same time, all of which ate into the limited laboratory and test bench resources.

The person at BMW with overall responsibility for rocket engine development was Helmut Graf von Zborowski.

The BMW rocket engines were unique, not only for the use of nitric acid as an oxidizer, but for other technological features as well. The cooled combustion chamber was made of metal alloy and exhibited a cylindrical combustion area. The entire rocket motor could be disassembled, consisted of simple to produce components, and the parts subject to wear were easy to replace with little time or effort involved.

The BMW method for feeding the rocket fuels using turbopumps was an idea that the Allies embraced and developed to its full potential after the war. One example of this was Hans Schneider (director of rocket development at BMW from 1943 to 1945 and deputy to Helmut Graf von Zborowski) who, with several of his former colleagues, went to work postwar at the French SEPR, where he worked on a rocket propulsion system for the SO 9000 *Trident* supersonic experimental plane.

Rheinmetall-Borsig
Starting in 1942 the company of Rheinmetall-Borsig AG at Berlin-Marienfelde began developing ballistic rocket projectiles and their associated powder-fuel rocket propulsion systems. This took place under the direction of Dr.-Ing. Hermann Vüllers. It was from these powder-fuel rocket engines that solid fuel rocket motors were derived, which were used as takeoff assistance for aircraft (e.g. the DFS 230).

RI 502
Takeoff booster rocket for aircraft with 1,000 kp initial thrust, with a burn time of six seconds. Diglycol powder was used as the fuel.

Schmidding
The Schmidding Company at Tetschen-Bodenbach carried out extensive experiments with cast diglycoldinitrate powder units as solid fuel rocket propulsion. The Schmidding powder rockets were mainly used as RATO boosters for aircraft.

A derivative of this principle was the development of a liquid fuel rocket motor (109-513) in cooperation with the Henschel Company for powering the Hs 293 and Hs 298 glide bombs. It burned methanol and pure oxygen as its fuel.

109-533
Diglycol-solid fuel takeoff booster rocket with a static thrust of 1,000 kp at a burn time of 12 seconds. The company designation of the system was the SG 34. Four of these units were used as auxiliary power for the Bachem Ba 349.

109-563
Diglycol-solid fuel takeoff booster with a static thrust of 500 kp at a burn time of six seconds.

109-503

Diglycol-solid fuel takeoff booster with a static thrust of 750 kp at a burn time of four seconds.

Westfälisch-Anhaltische Sprengstoff AG (WASAG)

The WASAG at Reinsdorf developed and built primarily powder propulsion systems for guided projectiles and military rockets for the Army and other branches of the armed forces.

109-522

Diglycol-solid fuel takeoff booster.

109-532

Diglycol-solid fuel takeoff booster, which was used in various transport gliders as a braking rocket as well.

Rocket Assisted Takeoff (RATO)

Junkers was the first in Germany to experiment with the use of rocket engines to improve takeoff performance for aircraft in 1929. The first attempt involved mounting two Eisfeld powder rockets beneath the fuselage of a W33/*See*. The rockets were to be ignited in tandem, giving a burn time of several seconds and a thrust of 75 kp.

The tests took place on the Elbe river, near Dessau. Company test pilot Zimmermann sat at the controls. On the initial attempt, one of the rockets exploded but did not cause any further damage. The second takeoff went more smoothly. But the disappointing thrust effect provided by the powder rockets used in the tests—which in all likelihood was due to imbalanced combustion—led to Junkers abandoning the experiments a short time later.

The first real functional liquid fuel rocket engines did not appear in Germany until just before the Second World War. The developments of Helmuth Walter

in Kiel and BMW have already been discussed in detail in the "Rocket Engines" chapter.

Without a doubt, the most developmentally advanced RATO booster based on a liquid fuel rocket system was the HWK 109-500 *Kraftei* and the HWK 109-501. These were produced in large numbers, and during the course of the war proved themselves to be virtually problem-free in over 3,000 takeoffs (with He 111s, Ju 88s, etc.). These two units were also known as *R-Geräte* (*Rauch-Geräte*, or "smoke systems"), and were designed to be completely self contained and jettisonable systems. They were in direct competition to the solid fuel boosters of the Schmidding company at Testchen-Bodenbach, Rheinmetall-Borsig at Belrin-Marienfelde, and the WASAG at Reinsdorf, with solid fuel rockets naturally being much easier to handle in the field than liquid fuel rockets.

When integrating RATO boosters into aircraft, it is of special importance that no part of the airframe be

Ju 88 with HWK 109-500 RATO pods. (*Bundesarchiv*)

Ju 88A taking off with the aid of two HWK 109-520 RATO pods. (*Bundesarchiv*)

affected by the hot exhaust gases from the rocket engine on the one hand, and on the other hand that the line of thrust be as close as possible to the center of drag to minimize any potential rolling motion.

The *Luftwaffe's* transport gliders were naturally the ideal candidates for the use/testing of rocket assisted takeoff boosters. The main focus here was to improve takeoff procedures, which were accomplished by means of one or more tow tugs. It was for this reason that experiments were done with all transport and assault gliders.

Go 242

Under the control of the DFL in Berlin, the test center in Rechlin carried out trials using RATO boosters on the Go 242 from the spring of 1942 until March of 1943. The tow tug in this case was a Heinkel He 111. For these tests, a special jettisonable frame was attached to the aft fuselage carrying four RI-502 powder rockets designed by Rheinmetall-Borsig, or alternatively an HWK 109-500 liquid fuel rocket unit was fitted beneath each wing close to the fuselage. The four RI-502 powder rockets were electrically ignited in se-

HWK 109-500 RATO pod beneath the wing of a Ju 88. (*Bundesarchiv*)

138

Me 321 taking off using RATO.

quence, each delivering 500 kp of thrust for six seconds. The program was terminated in March 1943 on the orders of the RLM. As a result of the tests, it was felt that the RI-502 powder rockets were better suited for use on the Go 242 because the aft frame offered less drag to a safe release altitude than the two underhung HWK 109-500 rocket pods.

DFS 230
Development of the DFS 230 began as early as 1936, with the aircraft being used in two different versions: as an assault glider for paratroopers and as a transport glider for carrying materials and troops. The aircraft became famous when, on 9 May 1940, German paratroopers attacked the Belgian fort of Eben-Emael on the Maas River. A total of 1,591 aircraft were built in different variants through to 1944.

The test center at Peenemünde-West began experiments using Rheinmetall-Borsig's RI-502 RATO booster with the DFS 230 in October 1942. These experiments had a two-fold purpose: to assess the operational reliability of the RI-502, and to determine the suitability and flight performance of RATO boosters for the DFS 230. Two static tests were successfully

carried out, but takeoff tests were a failure. As a result, clearance for the RI-502 units were temporarily put on hold.

In addition the DFS carried out special trials testing the viability of braking rockets in the nose of the DFS 230 C-1 assault glider variant. These were to have reduced the rollout distance to the point where landings would be possible in the most confined spaces (e.g. in mountainous terrain). In so doing, the braking delay would be limited to a maximum mass at the limits of toleration for the aircraft's occupants. The nose of the aircraft's fuselage was modified to accommodate three solid fuel rockets fitted into a triangular framework, which could be electrically ignited from the cockpit.

The first and probably only use of such a modified DFS 230 C-1 was in the rescue of Mussolini from Gran Sasso.

Me 321
Design work on the Me 321 began at Messerschmitt on 6 November 1940 and was based on a requirement for an aircraft capable of transporting a weight of 22 tons (Panzer II) over the English Channel. The

Me 321 with eight RATO pods attached.

aircraft's development was therefore directly linked to Operation *Seelöwe* (Sealion), the planned invasion of England. A total of 200 aircraft were built and stood ready in France until the invasion was canceled, at which point they were transferred to the Eastern Front.

Towed takeoff for this massive transport glider (wingspan: 55.24 m, length: 28.15 m, height: 10.15 m, empty weight: 12,100 kg, takeoff weight: 35,000 kg) posed particular problems. In all of Germany there

was only one airplane at the time capable of towing an Me 321 into the air. This was a Junkers Ju 90 with American engines. This Junkers Ju 90 was, in fact, the tow plane for the Me 321's first flight on 25 February 1941 at Obertraubling. However, it was discovered that even this plane was too underpowered for taking off with a fully loaded Me 321 in tow. As a result, for the sixth takeoff of the Me 321 V1 on 8 March 1941 it was decided to use the *Troika* tow method developed

Me 321 taking off under tow with the assistance of eight RATO motors. (photos: Radinger)

140

by the DFS, and beginning with the eighth takeoff this method was adopted as standard. The *Troika* tow involved three Messerschmitt Me 110s, tethered to the Me 321 via cables of different lengths, pulling the Me 321 to altitude. Depending on the Me 321's weight, additional boost was required in the form of RATO pods. A minimum of four and a maximum of eight HKW 109-500 RATO units, each with a thrust of 500 kp, were hung beneath the wings of the Me 321. This method was used successfully for the first time (in conjunction with the RATO boosters) on the Me 321 V2's third flight on 29 April 1941. The timing of the ignition sequence was naturally vitally important. The *Troika* tow itself carried a high degree of risk, as the tow planes had to tauten the cables and lift off simultaneously.

An effective solution was not found until the He 111Z was used as a tow plane. The He 111Z was made from two He 111-H6 airframes joined by a common center wing section that housed an additional Jumo 211-F2 engine. The first flight of the He 111Z took place on 14 January 1942. Depending on takeoff weight, the He 111Z-Me 321 team was supplemented

by up to 14 HWK 109-500 and 109-501 RATO booster rockets. Eight of the 109-500s were attached beneath the Me 321's wings, with a further two beneath each fuselage section of the He 111Z. An additional two 109-501 boosters were located beneath the He 111Z's outer wings. In this configuration, the Me 321 could carry a payload weighing 18,000 kg. These tests were carried out exclusively at the *Luftwaffe's* test center at Peenemünde West.

Messerschmitt developed an alternative to all these problems in the fall of 1941 in the form of a motorized variant (the Me 323), which was offered to the RLM. The Me 323 V1's first flight occurred in the spring of 1942. HWK RATO boosters could also be fitted to the Me 323 in overloaded conditions.

Other clients for the use of assisted takeoff rockets included the *Luftwaffe's* first generation of turbojet powered aircraft designs. Jettisonable RATO pods were an ideal way to considerably reduce the rather long takeoff runs, thereby virtually eliminating the Achilles' heel of these valuable planes. Trials focused particular attention on the Me 262 and Ar 234 aircraft types.

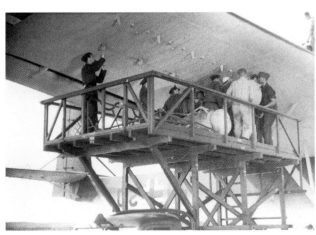

Above: Fitting RATO units onto the Me 321. Following page: Me 323 with eight RATO pods fitted.

As early as July 1943 Arado proposed a twinjet Ar 234A reconnaissance version using two HWK 109-500 RATO boosters, one beneath each outer wing section, in addition to the turbojet engines. This configuration was tested for the first time using the Ar 234 V2 on 13 September 1943, and was later frequently in use. However, beginning in 1944 there were problems with the availability of the special hydrogen peroxide fuel, which at this time was reserved exclusively for the Me 163 aircraft. Experiments with RATO boosters on the Me 262 have already been described in detail in the chapter on the Me 262 Interceptor and will therefore not be covered further here.

Appendices

Abbreviations Index

I./JG 400	I. Gruppe Jagdgeschwader 400 (1 Group Fighter Wing 400)
1./JG 400	1. Staffel Jagdgesschwader 400 (1 Squadron Fighter Wing 400)
AFB	Air Force Base
Ar	Arado (company name)
AVA	Aerodynamische Versuchsanstalt (Aerodynamic Test Center)
Ba	Bachem (company name)
BK	Bordkanoneb (onboard cannon)
BMW	Bayerische Motorenwerke (company name)
BP	Bachem Project
Bramo	Brandenburgische Motorenwerke (company name)
C-Stoff	rocket fuel (30% hydrazine hydrate, 57% methanol, 13% water, plus traces of calium copper cyanide and hypergol with H_2O_2)
DB	Daimler-Benz (company name)
DFS	Deutsches Forschungsinstitut für Segelflug (German Sailplane Research Institute)
Do	Dornier (company name)
DVL	Deutsche Versuchsanstalt für Luftfahrt (German Experimental Aviation Institute)
EK	Erprobungskommando
E-Stelle	Erprobungsstelle (test/evaluation center)
FFG	Flugtechnische Fachgruppe
Ki	Fieseler (company name)
FuG	Funkgerät (radio equipment)
Fw	Feldwebel (sergeant/non-commissioned officer)
Fw	Focke-Wulf (company name)
Go	Gothaer Waggonfabrik (company name)
He	Heinkel (company name)
Hptm	Hauptmann (captain)
HWA	Heereswaffenamt (Army Office of Weapons)
HWK	Hellmuth Walter Kommanditgesellschaft (company name)
Ju	Junkers (company name)
KG	Kampfgeschwader (bomber wing)
Kl	Klemm (company name)
LFW	Luftfahrtforschungsanstalt Wien (Aviation Research Institute, Vienna)
Lt	Leutnant (lieutenant)
Me	Messerschmitt (company name)
MG	Maschinengewehr (machine gun)
MK	Maschinenkanone (machine cannon)
NACA	National Advisory Committee for Aeronautics (today's NASA)
Olt	Oberleutnant (first lieutenant)
OSA	Oberstabsarzt (senior staff doctor)
RAE	Royal Aircraft Establishment
Rb	Reihenbildgerät (camera)
RLM	Reichsluftfahrtministerium (Imperial Ministry of Aviation)
RRG	Rhön-Rossitten-Gesellschaft (company name)
SG	Sondergerät (special equipment)
SO	Selbstopferung (self-sacrifice/suicide)
TH	Technische Hochschule (technical school)
TL	Turboluftstrahl (turbojet)
T-Stoff	rocket fuel (80% hydrogen peroxide)
Twk	Triebwerk (engine)
WASAG	Westfälische Anhaltische Sprengstoff AG (company name)

Conversion Table
Physical Units

1kp	9.80665 N
1 kg	9.80665 N
1 lbs	0.454 kg
1 ft	0.3048 m
1 nm	1,852 m
1 PS	0.7355 kW
1 hp	1.0139 PS
1 kg/kph	101,972 kg/kNh
1 bar	0.1 N/mm^2
1 mbar	100 N/m^2
1 bar	1.0197 kp/cm^2

1 N/mm^2 145.038 psi

Speeds

	m/s	km/h	ft/s	ft/min	kt
m/s	1	3.6	3.2808	196.85	1.9438
km/h	0.2778	1	0.9113	54.68	0.5310
ft/s	0.3048	1.0973	1	60.0	0.5925
ft/min	0.00508	0.0183	0.0167	1	0.00987
kt	0.5144	1.8520	1..6878	101.27	1

Constants

gravity	g=9.80665 m/s
speed of sound in air	c=340 m/s (at 20% C and normal pressure)

Sources

Heinz J. Nowarra: "Die deutsche Luftrüstung 1933-1945", Bernard & Graefe Verlag

Willy Radinger/Walter Schick: "Me 262"; Aviatic Verlag

Hans-Peter Diedrich: "Die deutschen Strahlflugzeuge bis 1945"; Aviatic Verlag

Anonymous: "Heinkel - Chronik und Typenblätter"; Aviatic Verlag

Otto E. Pabst: "Kurzstarter und Senkrechtstarter"; Bernard & Graefe Verlag

Kyrill von Gersdorff/Kurt Grasmann: "Flugmotoren und Strahltriebwerke"; Bernard & Graefe Verlag

Hans J. Ebert/ Johann B. Kaiser/ Klaus Peters: "Willy Messerschmitt - Pionier der Luftfahrt und des Leichtbaus"; Bernard & Graefe Verlag

Hans-Peter Dabrowski: "Jagdeinsitzer He 112"; Waffen-Arsenal Volume 159

Eric Brown: "Berühmte Flugzeuge der Luftwaffe 1939-1945"; Motorbuch Verlag

B. Johnson: "Streng Geheim -Wissenschaft und Technik im Zweiten Weltkrieg"; Paul Pietsch Verlage GmbH, Stuttgart

Mano Ziegler: "Kampf um Mach 1"; EHAPA Verlag

J.L. Ethell: "Messerschmitt Komet"; Motorbuch Verlag

Joachim Dressel/Manfred Griehl: "Die deutschen Raketenflugzeuge 1935-1945"; Motorbuch Verlag

Volkhard Bode/Gerhard Kaiser: "Raketenspuren"; Bechtermünz Verlag

Theodor Benecke/Karl-Heinz Hedwig/Joachim Hermann: "Flugkörper und Lenkraketen"; Bernard & Graefe Verlag

Ludwig Bölkow: "Ein Jahrhundert Flugzeuge"; VDI Verlag

H. Dieter Köhler: "Ernst Heinkel - Pionier der Schnellflugzeuge"; Bernard & Graefe Verlag

Rüdiger Kosin: "Die Entwicklung der deutschen Jagdflugzeuge"; Bernard & Graefe Verlag

Kurt W. Streit/John W.R. Taylor: "Geschichte der Luftfahrt"; Sigloch Service Edition

Helmut Schubert: "Deutsche Triebwerke"; Aviatic Verlag

Bruno Lange: "Das Buch der deutschen Luftfahrttechnik"; Verlag Dieter Hoffmann

Eugen Sänger: "Raumfahrt"; Econ-Verlag

Anonymous: "Die schnellsten Flugzeuge der Welt"; Flugrevue 2/98

Wolfdietrich Hoeveler: "Space Shuttle 0 Das einzige Flugzeug im All"; Flugrevue 2/98

Christopher Hess: "X-33 - Technologieträger für das nächste Space Shuttle"; Flugrevue 3/99

Christopher Hess: "Europas Raumfähre"; Flugrevue 7/99

Christopher Hess: "Neue Wege ins All"; Flugrevue 12/99

Karl R. Pawlas: "Projekt Flitzer"; Luftfahrt International No. 17

Karl R. Pawlas: "Me 163 - Das letzte Aufgebot"; Luftfahrt International No. 9

Karl R. Pawlas: "Bachem Natter"; Luftfahrt International No. 10

Karl R. Pawlas: "Kampf- und Lastensegler DFS 230/DFS 331"; Luftfahrt Monographie LS 1

Karl R. Pawlas: "Die Sturm- und Lastensegler Go 242, Go 244, Go 345, P39, Ka 430"; Luftfahrt Monographie LS 2

Karl R. Pawlas: "Die Giganten Me 321/Me 323"; Luftfahrt Monographie LS 3

Karl R. Pawlas: "Arado Ar 234 -Der erste Strahlbomber der Welt"; Luftfahrt Dokumente LD21

Georg Brüttling: "Das Buch der deutschen Fluggeschichte"; Drei Brunnen Verlag

Wolfgang Wagner: "Kurt Tank - Konstrukteur und Testpilot bei Focke-Wulf"; Bernard & Graefe Verlag

A. Lippisch/Fr. Stamer: "Raketenversuche mit Flugzeugen und Flugzeugmodellen"; Zeitschrift für Flugtechnik und Motorluftschifffahrt 12/1928

Photo Credits
I wish to thank the following persons and institutions for their permission to make use of their photographs:

Mr. Lothar Nebgen
Mr. Willy Radinger
Deutsches Museum, Munich
DaimlerChrysler Aerospace
MTU Motoren- und Turbinenunion GmbH
Luftwaffen Museum, Berlin-Gatow
Adam Opel AG, Rüsselsheim
Bundesarchiv

Furthermore, my thanks goes out to the Deutsches Technikmuseum, Berlin, and the Deutsches Segelflugmuseum for their helpful support in the search for material.

And finally, I owe a debt of gratitude to my family for their manifest understanding while they had to put up with my all too frequent absences during the research and preparation of the book.

Technical Overview

Name	Type	Crew	Wingspan (m)	Length (m)	Height (m)	Engine	Performance (Kp)	vmax (km/h)	at altitude of (m)	empty weight (kg)	full weight (kg)	armament
Ar 234 R	R	1	14.41	12.65	4.42	1 x HWK109-509C	2,000 + 400	915	17,000	3,500	7,100	aerial photography cameras
Ar 234C	C	1	14.41	12.65	4.42	2 x BMW 003A and 2 x BMW 003R	4x 800 + 2 x 1,250	960				
Ar E381	C	1	5.00	5.70	-	1 x MWK 109-509C	400	900	8,000	745	1,200 65173	2 x MG 131 and R4M or RZ
Ba 349A	C	1	3.60	5.72	2.20	1 x HWK 109-509 A-2 + 2 x SG 34	1,700 + 2 x 1,200	1,000	800		2,050	24 x *Föhn* or 33 x R4M or 49 x SG119
Ba 349B	C	1	4.00	6.02	2.225	1 x HWK 109-509 A-2 + 4 x SG 34	1,700 + 4 x 1,200	1,000	1,095		2,270	24 x *Föhn* or 2 x MK 108
DFS 194	E	1	9.30	7.20		1 x HWK RI-203	400	550	0		2,100	none
DFS 228	R	1	17.55	10.50		1 x HWK 109-509 A-1	1,600	900	-	1,350	4,210	none
DFS 346	E	1	8.98	11.65	3.50	2 x HWK 109-509 B-1	w x 2,000	2,270[1]	20,000	-	5,200	none
Fw *Flitzer*	C	1	8.00	10.55	2.35	1 x Heinkel HeS 011	1,300+1,900	925	9,000	3,068	4,820	2 x MK 108 and 2 x MG 151/20
He 112R-V2	E	1	9.10	9.30	3.80	1 x DB600A and 1 x *Aggregat I*	960 hp + 300 kp					none
He 176	E	1	5.00	5.20	1.44	1 x HWK RI-203	600	750	4,000	900	1,620	none
He P.1077 *Julia*	C	1	4.60	6.80	1.50	1 x HWK 109-509 A-2	1,700 + 300	970	5,000	956	1,795	2 x MK 108
Ju EF 127	C	1	6.65	7.60	-	1 x HWK 109-509 A-2	1,700 + 300	950	-	1,030	2,960	2 x MG 151/200 or MG 213 + 12 *Panzerblitz* launch racks
Me 163B-1	C	1	9.30	5.70	2.50	1 x HWK 109-509 A-1	1,600	900	-	1980	4,310	2 x MK 108
Me 163C	C	1	9.80	7.04		1 x HWK 109-509 A-2	1,700 + 300	950	-	2,200	5,000	2 x MK 108
Me 263/Ju 248	C	1	9.50	7.89	-	1 x HWK 109-509c	2,000 + 400	950	6,000	2,21-	5,300	2 x MK 108
Me 262 C-1a	C	1	12.50	10.60	3.83	2 x Jumo 004 B-1 + 1 x HWK 109-509S	2 x 900 + 1 x 1,700	873	6,000	4,000	6,775	4 x MK 108
Me 262 C-2b	C	1	12.50	10.60	3.83	2 x BMW 003A-1 + 2 x BMW 109-718	2 x 800 = 2 x 1,200	750	6,000	4,000	7,090	4 x MK 108
Me P1104	C	1		5.48		1 x HWK 109-509 A-2	1,700 + 300	800	-	-	2,540	1 x MK 108

149

Legend:
R = reconnaissance aircraft C=combat aircraft E=experimental aircraft

Notes:
[1]theoretical

Rocket Engines and RATO Booster Rocekts (*R-Geräte*)

RLM designation	Manufacturer designation	Thrust (kp)	Combustion chambers	Burn time (s)	Fuel	Weight (kg)	Length (m)	Diameter (m)	Manufacturer	Usage
	R1-203	600	1	60	hydrogen peroxide and methanol *T-Stoff, Z-Stoff* controllable				HWK	He 176 propulsion
	RII-203	150-750	1						HWK	Me 163A propulsion
109-500A	R1-203A	500	1	30	hydrogen peroxide plus catalyst		1.42	0.68	HWK	DFS 194 propulsion
109-501	R1-203B	1,500	1		hydrogen peroxide, petroleum with catalyst	250 (L.)			HWK	RATO for He 111, Ju 88, Ju 287
109-502	R1 202B	1,000	1	6	hydrazine hydrate and catalyst; same as 109-501	250 (B)			Rheinmetall / HWK	*Enzian* E1 propulsion
109-503		1,000	1	43	same as 109-501				HWK	RATO (small prototype series)
109-505		500	2	6	diglycol	48 (total)	1.27	0.178	Rheinmetall	F25 *Feuerlilie* and Me 262 (experimental) propulsion
109-506		70.5		3.8	diglycol				WASAG	two-stage propulsion for the X-7
109-507	RII 260/I-4	585-600	1	10	hydrogen peroxide, *Z-Stoff*				HWK	Hs 293-294 and 295 propulsion
109-509 A-0	RII-211/1	300-1,500 controllable			hydrogen peroxide, *C-Stoff*	175	2.5		HWK	Me 163 B and *Eber* tow fighter propulsion
109-509 A-1	RII 211/2	100-1,600 controllable			same as 109-509A-0				HWK	Me 163 B-0, Ba 349 and DFS 228 propulsion
109-509 A-2	RII 211	300 constant plus 200-1,700 controllable	2		same as 109-509 A-0	180			HWK	Me 163C propulsion
109-509 B	RII 211	100-2,000 controllable	1		same as 109-509A-0				HWK	Me 163 B-1 and Ar E381 propulsion
109-509 C	RII-211	400 constant plus 400-2,000 controllable	2		same as 109-509 A-0				HWK	Me 163C and Me 253 (Ju 248) propulsion
109-509 D	RII-211	400 constant plus 400-2,000 controllable	2		same as 109-509 A-0				HWK	Ba 349 B propulsion
109-S for DFS 228 propulsion	RII 211/3	200-1,700 controllable	1		same as 109-509 A-0				HWK	derivative of 109-509 A-2
109-510	P3390	300-1,500 controllable	1	33-90	methanol, *Sv-Stoff*	140			BMW	Me 163 B and Me 163 C propulsion
109-511	P3374 RII 302	600	1	12	methanol, *Sv-Stoff*	98			BMW	Hs 293 A and Hs 298 propulsion

Designation	Type	Thrust (kp)	Stages	Propellant	Burn time (sec)	Weight (kg)	Manufacturer	Application / Notes
109-512		1,000	1	diglycol	10		WASAG	Hs 293 GV propulsion
109-513		1,000	1	oxygen, methanol	10			Schmidding Hs 209 and Hs 298 propulsion (alternate)
109-515		4,000	1	diglycol	6		Rheinmetall	F55 *Feuerlilie* and Hs 293 V2 propulsion
109-519				diglycol			Rheinmetall	solid fuel rocket propulsion
109-522				diglycol			WASAG	solid fuel RATO booster
109-528	P3377						BMW	BV LT L 1000b propulsion
109-532	RI-502 B			diglycol			WASAG	Me 262 B-2a, He 162 and Ba 349 RATO booster, braking system for the DFS 230, tested for the Hs 293
109-533	SG34	1,000	1	diglycol	12	120 (total)		Schmidding RATO booster for Me 262 B-2a, Me 163, Ba 349 and propulsion for Hs 293 FV1-3
109-543	SG32	150 and 50	1	diglycol	5 and 12			Schmidding two-stage solid fuel propulsion for the Hs 298 and Hs 293
109-548	P3378	140 kp thrust dropping to 30 kp	1	*Tonka, Sv-Stoff*	22	13.5 (empty) 8.5 (fuel)		BMW X4 propulsion: 1,300 units produced
109-553		1,750	1	diglycol	4		Schmidding	Enzian E1 and Hs 117 propulsion and Ba 349 RATO booster
109-558	P3386	60-380 controllable	1	*Tonka, Sv-Stoff*	33-90	180 (total)		BMW Hs 117 propulsion; approx. 125 units built
109-559		150-1,700 controllable		hydrogen peroxide, *C-Stoff*			HWK	simplified propulsion system for the Ba 349A
109-563		500	1	diglycol	6		Schmidding	solid fuel RATO booster for Me 262A and B
109-573				diglycol			Schmidding	solid fuel underwater propulsion system
109-593		750	1	diglycol	4		Schmidding	solid fuel RATO booster
109-603		150	1	diglycol	8		Schmidding	X4 propulsion
109-708	P3390 C	100-2,500 controllable	2	*Tonka, Sv-Stoff*	35	210	BMW	Me 163 C; small numbers built in 1945

Model	Designation	Thrust / Power	Chambers	Running time	Propellant	Mass	Manufacturer	Remarks
109-718	P3395	1,250	1	180	*Tonka, Sv-Stoff*	80	BMW	Me 262 C-2b and Ar 234 R (BMW 109-003 TLR); about 35 units built
109-729		375 kp thrust after 10 s dropping to 60 kp	1	10; 60	*Tonka, Sv-Stoff*	150 (empty)	HWK	Hs 117 propulsion
109-739		2,000 kp initial thrust dropping to 1,000 kp	1	69	*Visol, Sv-Stoff*		Konrad	Enzian E4 propulsion
RI 502		1,000	1	6	diglycol		Rheinmetall	RATO booster
RI 301	P-3370	1,000	1	30	hydrogen peroxide, methanol/ hydrazine hydrate	420 (total)	BMW	RATO booster for Ju 88; 10 prototypes built
	P-3371	1,000			same as P-3370		BMW	RATO booster for Ju 88; project
RI 305	P-3372	1,500	1	45	*Tonka, Sv-Stoff*	645	BMW	RATO booster for Ju 88; project
RI 302	P-3373	1,500	1	45	methanol, *Sv-Stoff*	650	BMW	RATO booster for Ju 88; three prototypes built
RII 301	P-3375	1,500	1	10	*Tonka, Sv-Stoff*	178	BMW	Hs 294 propulsion; project
	P-3376	1,500, 300	2	20+40	*Tonka, Sv-Stoff*	515	BMW	two-stage glide bomb propulsion; project
	P-3377	2 x 185 kW	1	240	*Tonka, Sv-Stoff*	150	BMW	LT1000 torpedo propulsion; project
	P-3378	1,000	1	60	*Tonka, Sv-Stoff*		BMW	Bv 143 glide bomb; project
	P-3379	2,000	1	20.5	methanol, *Sv-Stoff*		BMW	Me 163 takeoff trolley propulsion; project
	P-3380	1,000	1		benzine, liquid oxygen		BMW	aerial torpedo propulsion; project
	P-3381	500	1	50	*Tonka, Sv-Stoff*		BMW	catapult propulsion; project
	P-3382	45,000			*Tonka, Sv-Stoff*	370	BMW	propulsion for propeller with engines on blades; project
	P-3385	1,750 kW			*Tonka, Sv-Stoff*		BMW	glide bomber propulsion; project
RII 260	none	600	1	12	*Tonka, Sv-Stoff*		BMW	glide bomber propulsion; project

HWK   Hellmuth Walter Kiel
WASAG   Westfälisch-Anhaltsche Sprengstoff AG in Reinsdorf
Rheinmetall   Rheinmetall-Borsig in Berlin-Marienfelde

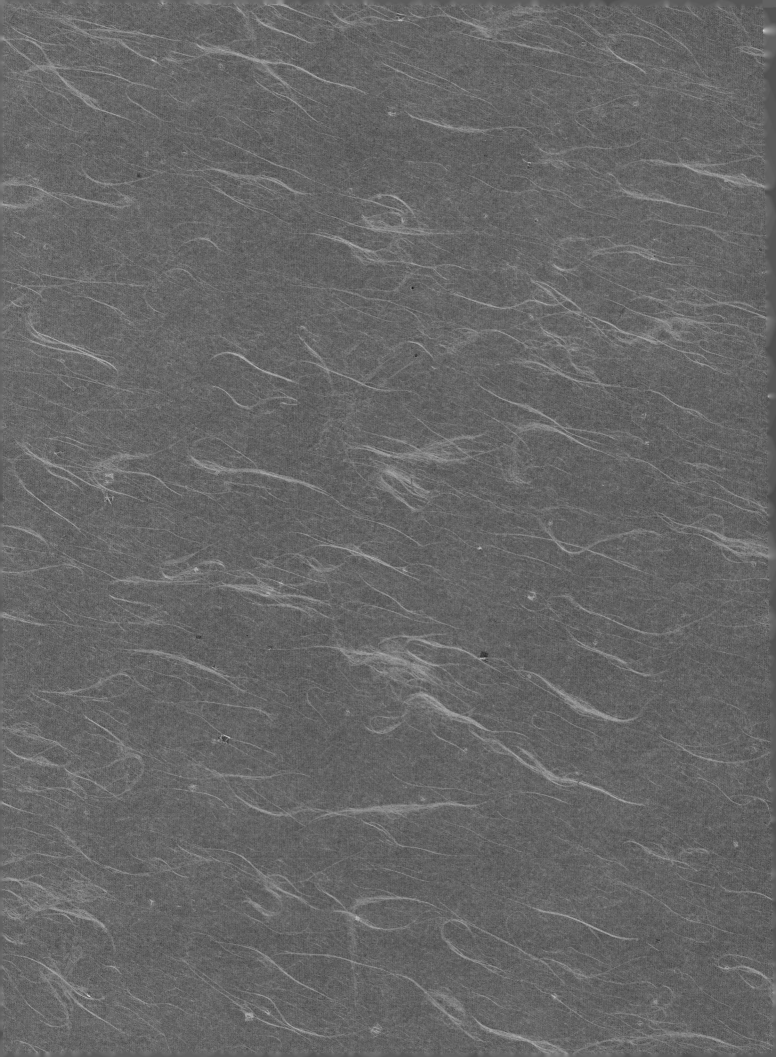